"We've been trying your eating method with our daughter, Jessica. After a few days of 'chocolate popsicles' she decided she wanted chicken and broccoli for dinner. *Believe me*, she has never asked for a green vegetable—*ever!!*"

Susan Leonard
Parent

"Kids generally are not fat because of what they we let them eat, but because of what we don't let them eat. Jane Hirschmann's and Lela Zaphiropoulos's book has given me a way to illustrate this fact to parents, allowing me to help them and their children out of the diet trap."

Dana U. Armstrong, R.D.
Clinical Nutritionist

"This approach has alleviated the conflict between my daughter and myself. Our relationship has changed and I am no longer judging her. It's taken the pressure off."

Debra Short
Parent

"An ounce of prevention worth pounds of cure. It shows all parents how to reduce the conflicts surrounding food and feelings and makes clear the importance of building with a healthy relationships to food early on, *before* it becomes a problem."

Jeffrey H. Sacks, D. O.
Director of Child Psychiatry
St. Lukes-Roosevelt Hospital

SOLVING YOUR CHILD'S EATING PROBLEMS

FORMERLY TITLED *ARE YOU HUNGRY?*

A COMPLETELY NEW APPROACH TO RAISING CHILDREN FREE OF FOOD AND WEIGHT PROBLEMS

Jane R. Hirschmann
and Lela Zaphiropoulos

Introduction by
William B. Bateman, Jr., M.D.

Fawcett Columbine · New York

A Fawcett Columbine Book
Published by Ballantine Books

Library of Congress Catalog Card Number: 89-91514

ISBN 0-449-90512-0

Cover design by Sheryl Kagan

Manufactured in the United States of America
First Ballantine Books Edition: July 1990
10 9 8 7 6 5 4 3 2 1

To the women
whose work so greatly influenced our ideas:

Carol Munter
Susie Orbach

To the children
who taught us that these ideas were right:

Jesse Gilbert
Kate Hirschmann-Levy
Nell Hirschmann-Levy
Leta Hirschmann-Levy

To the men
whose love and encouragement sustained us:

Richard A. Levy
Jan Van Assen

ACKNOWLEDGMENTS

We owe a great deal to Carol Munter and Susie Orbach, psychotherapists and feminist thinkers, for their pioneering work. Together they developed an analysis of women's obsession with food, eating and body size along with a treatment approach demonstrating that people can be free of eating problems without diet and food restrictions. It is their ground-breaking work that inspired our thinking about the way children eat and families deal with feeding.

There have been many people along the way who have helped us in our work. We are deeply grateful:

Carol Bloom, over a decade ago, gave us the impetus to work with women with compulsive eating problems. The New School for Social Research and Nancy Samalin of Parent Guidance Workshops provided us with the first forums to discuss our ideas about self-demand feeding for children. Many parents who attended these sessions gave rich anecdotal material for this book.

In the beginning stages, Dr. Cynthia Carver encouraged us to write this book, constructively challenged our ideas and helped us organize the material. Bill Ayers, Bernardine Dohrn, Luise Eichenbaum, Karen Levine, Ronnie Littenberg and Liz Werby read and offered valuable comments on the manuscript. Lucy Gilbert gave helpful advice on the process of writing a book. Jan Van Assen's knowledge about society and culture added to this book's perspective. And, in various private ways, thanks are due Augusta Zaphiropoulos-Barnet, Dr. Miltiades Zaphiropoulos and Dr. Edith Schwartz.

Ellen Levine, our agent, guided this book through to completion. Her availability, frankness and friendship were a steadying force. Charlotte Mayerson, our editor, with remarkable skills and enormous energy, worked with us beyond the call of duty.

Finally, we would like to give special acknowledgment to:
Carol Munter, who shared a wealth of information based on her professional experience dealing with compulsive eaters. She carefully read each chapter in progress and helped us strengthen the clarity of our vision.

Richard A. Levy, who sacrificed so much of his time and energy reworking drafts of our manuscript. His insistence on precision and detail as well as his compassion and humor were invaluable.

CONTENTS

INTRODUCTION

It is my pleasure to welcome you to a very important book. Important because of its audience, families with children; its subject, healthy eating; and its perspective, that healthy family eating practices are enjoyable.

But do not look for diets or recipes. They are not in this book. The authors believe, as I do, that despite the fact that "new" diets still appear regularly on the best-seller list, they are almost never truly new and rarely improve our understanding or our practice of healthful nutrition.

The emphasis here is far more relevant and enduring. The authors are describing a method that parents can use to help their children accomplish what so many of us, as adults, have been unable to achieve—the ability to eat in a way that is satisfying *and* healthful.

The method or program is simple to remember. It is sensibly presented. Its application is well illustrated with anecdotes covering infancy through adolescence. Particular problems posed by eating disorders—anorexia, bulimia and compulsive overeating—and special diets are also covered. The anecdotes and accounts of individual families allow the reader to develop a sense of the program's practical application.

What is the program? The authors urge us to establish three principles in order to help our children develop good eating habits. First, they should eat when they are physically hungry and *only* when they are hungry. Second, they themselves should have the responsibility for determining the foods they eat. And finally, they should stop eating when they feel full.

Is this kitchen anarchy? Is it children's rights gone crazy? No, but the book must be read and discussed to understand and apply these innovative principles.

Can the program be trusted? Why should we believe the authors?

I am a specialist and teacher in the diagnosis and medical treatment of adults, a teaching and practicing internist. I am also a father and husband. In each of these activities, I am keenly interested in nutrition and its impact on health and disease. I did not always have this interest, but experience has taught, and is teaching me that while the statement "We are what we eat" can be taken too literally, it contains far more truth than fiction.

At the same time, I have learned that knowing what a proper diet is is not the same as actually *eating* one. All sorts of things get in the way: personal finances, cooking and shopping skills, work, the home situation and, most important, our individual food desires and our problems with self-control.

I believe in the authors' program because it helps children develop self-control rather than relying on others to tell them what to eat. Consider the difference between someone who says, "My doctor, mother, father, or spouse wants me to quit smoking," and someone who says, "I want to quit smoking."

As a physician who is interested in good nutrition and good eating habits, I feel this book is unusually worthwhile. I also believe in the program because I have seen the benefit in my own children and our family life.

The experience and credentials of the authors provide additional reasons to accept the program as safe and effective. Both are therapists with extensive experience working with adults, children and families concerned with eating well. Their book is likely to initiate a learning experience for you and your family that will enrich your life and benefit your children.

William B. Bateman, Jr., M.D.
Director, Internal Medicine
      Training Program of the
      Residency Program in
      Social Medicine,
      Montefiore Medical Center
Assistant Professor in the
      Departments of Internal
      Medicine, and Epidemiology
      and Social Medicine,
      Albert Einstein College
      of Medicine

I

THE PROGRAM

THE FOOD AND WEIGHT PROBLEM

Most of us are constantly concerned with food: what we eat; how much we eat; how it's cooked; where we're eating; at what time. Along with this goes the preoccupation with what food is doing to us: Is it making us fat? making us "hyperactive"? raising our cholesterol? upsetting our stomachs? giving us acne?

Such questions take up a lot of time and energy. Though we may not be obsessed with them, still, the problems of food and weight nag at most of us more than we would like. Particularly in families with children, eating becomes the sore spot, the cause of quarrels, dinnertime turmoil, jealousy, tension, over- and under-indulgences . . . . How many of us remember feeling insulted when food we lovingly prepared for our child was rejected? Or badgering a child to eat her vegetables before having dessert? Or worrying about a child who ate too much or too little?

Probably, in fact, we also remember similar confrontations with our own parents when *we* were children. As a result we ourselves grew up far from comfortable in our relationship to food. The cycle can be never ending. We have problems with food; we pass them on to our children. And yet, in our work in this field for the past eighteen years, we've seen families break away—putting eating, weight and rules about food into a new perspective that freed them to live a different kind of life.

Our professional work has been with adults who are compulsive eaters or with parents who have problems with their children over food and weight. But the fact is, there is hardly any parent who hasn't, at one time or another, worried about the subject. And most of us have wished it were possible to raise our children free of the national obsession with food, eating and body size.

This book introduces a program that we have seen accomplish this goal time and time again. Our approach is a natural and common sense way to feed your child, not just in infancy, but from birth through adolescence. It proceeds from the idea that the body is self-regulatory and children should eat only when they are hungry, eat only foods of their own choosing, and stop eating when *they* feel full. The numerous rules, rituals, schedules and myths that have nothing to do with the natural purpose of food are eliminated.

To questions like, "Why can't I eat my dessert first?" "Why do I have to have breakfast?" "Why can't I eat all my Halloween candy?" you can answer, "No reason at all. You can." And this answer doesn't lead to ill health, chaos, a loss of family discipline or any other disaster. In fact, good parenting requires this answer because it leads to "self-demand feeding," the one approach that discourages excesses and obsessions around food. That's what this book is about.

Our purpose is to help you break many time-worn rules that have interfered with your child's ability to be self-regulatory. It's our experience that life can be much easier with self-demand feeding because it allows you to give up unnecessary control and the concomitant struggles over food. Eating becomes more enjoyable, feeding tasks are simplified, and family members are able to untangle emotional issues from feeding issues.

We know that many parents are concerned with *what* their children eat—additives, sugar, cholesterol . . . . This book does not tell you what to feed your child, but rather presents an approach to these issues. Children raised with self-demand feeding are much more open to hearing and accepting sound information about food because they don't perceive parental advice as a contest of wills. Instead they understand that it is information they need to help them decide for themselves what to eat. That's the key—the child knows he or she will make the final decision.

Furthermore, children on this approach will eat more satisfyingly because they will be closely in touch with their bodies' signals. They will eat nutritiously because their natural appetite will call for the full range of food elements that are necessary for healthy growth and development.

There are three sections to this book:

Book I, "The Program," gives a detailed explanation of self-demand feeding and provides a step-by-step guide to introducing it in your home.

Book II, "From Year to Year," explains more specifically how to apply self-demand feeding by age groups from birth through adolescence. It describes how food and eating issues arise at various stages and how they can be minimized or corrected. Even though you may first turn to those chapters representing your children's specific ages, spend some time reading the other material in this section. You may find that your six-year-old's behavior is described in the four-year-old section or that your ten-year-old is already going through the Turbulent Teens.

In Book III, "Special Problems," we discuss eating disorders as well as certain medical difficulties that may influence eating. We have seen self-demand feeding used successfully even where food problems and restrictions exist.

> Remember that the approach described in this book is geared to the average child *with no medical problems*. If you have a child with any medical condition, consult your physician about diet and this program. Modifications can be made with self-demand feeding even though this is not the main thrust of our book.

2

DISPELLING THE MYTHS

In every culture the subject of food is surrounded by myths and rituals. For example, "Don't go in the water right after you've eaten" may make some sense. But we have found that, generally speaking, these "truths" turn out not to be sensible guidelines but rather obstacles in the way of happy and healthy eating. Let's look at some of the common ones:

Myth: If You Eat Now, You'll Spoil Your Appetite

Eleven-year-old Joyce, in the midst of doing her homework, feels hungry. She goes to the kitchen, where her mother is preparing dinner, and begins rummaging through the shelves and the refrigerator. As she selects crackers and cheese, her mother says, "Don't eat *now*, you'll spoil your appetite. I'm making dinner and we'll eat in half an hour when Daddy gets home."

"Don't spoil your appetite" is a refrain heard by each generation of growing children. What does it mean? How can anyone "spoil" an appetite by eating? Appetite is an internal signal; hunger pangs indicate a need for food. Eating satisfies, it does not spoil, an appetite. What parents really mean when they say, "Don't spoil your appetite," is that the child should stifle her appetite—her natural feelings of hunger. They mean, "Don't eat when you want to, eat when I want you to." The warning tells a child that she should not eat *now* because eating when she is hungry is eating out of turn. She should wait and eat when the meal is ready.

If a half an hour before dinner, Joyce feels hungry and wants cheese and crackers, what's the problem? At that moment Joyce's body is calling out for food. Her internal time clock is different from her mother's. Can Joyce trust her own signals or should she just suppress them and wait out the half hour? Consistent use of "Don't eat now, you'll spoil your appetite" confuses the child. It puts her in physical discomfort, makes her doubt the validity of her natural feelings, causes feelings of guilt because her needs are in conflict with her mother's wishes. And it often leads to needless struggles between parent and child. The child who has to wait too long will be so hungry that she may overeat at dinner, unable to recognize fullness when it comes. It is difficult to know when you are full if you sit down to eat feeling "starved."

This book will show you that it is perfectly okay if Joyce eats when she is hungry, even if it means eating less at dinner or eating no dinner at all. She will thrive; she will learn to eat when hungry and stop when full; and you will be free of the endless struggle that comes when artificial eating schedules are imposed.

Myth: If You Eat That, You'll Ruin Your Appetite

Imagine that you have just cooked an elaborate dinner of foods you know your children love. Your seven-year-old son declares that he wants bread and nothing else. You are annoyed. You spent a long time preparing what you thought was his favorite meal—meat loaf, peas and potatoes. What is the matter with him anyway? He wants bread and you think he should eat "dinner."

His love for the foods you have cooked has not necessarily

diminished. It's only that he wants something else right now. Can anyone know exactly which food will meet a child's internal hunger need *at the moment?* Think back. Haven't you found yourself in this or a similar situation: Your partner brings home lamb chops and wants to surprise you by barbecuing them just the way you love them best. Unfortunately, you are in the mood for some pasta or a salad. Even though you love barbecued lamb chops, that's not what you feel hungry for now. Perhaps you had meat for lunch or too big a lunch to be ready for another heavy meal. You, too, are selective about what you want to eat and cannot always enjoy what someone else desires. If your child says he wants bread when you want him to eat "dinner" foods, he is expressing the same feelings.

Even though the parents' intentions are good, interfering is risky. First, the pleasure of eating can be taken from the child. You get this pleasure from eating what you're hungry for. When a child is repeatedly told that his food desires are not correct or will not be met, there is little joy in eating. Second, the constant message that what the child feels he needs does not matter can be a great source of pain and confusion. Indeed, that message can damage his feelings of self-worth. Third, the instruction "Don't eat that," like the instruction "Don't eat now," keeps the child from learning to respond to his own signals of when he's hungry and what food will satisfy him. Fourth, this kind of interference invariably creates needless conflict in the family over who is eating what. As most of us have learned, battles over eating have no winners.

Can you believe that left to his own choices your child will eat all that is necessary for healthy growth? He will!

Myth: Balanced Meals Are Necessary for Good Health

Another common mealtime scenario goes something like this: Mother has prepared meat loaf, peas and potatoes. Joyce helps herself to potatoes only, and then her mother tells her that it is important to eat a balanced meal. Her mother is caught up in one of our major food myths: To stay healthy, every meal must be balanced. *Wrong!* Nutritional science and new research have made it clear that one to two weeks, not one meal or even one day, is the time frame within which the body needs to receive and absorb the range of nutrients necessary for healthy growth and development. This makes a strong case for allowing children to eat foods of their own choosing when they're hungry. Joyce may have a potato at dinner and protein later on, fruits or vegetables the next day and so on. In a week's time she will have eaten a balanced diet on her own schedule.

Another popular myth that takes the idea of a balanced meal one step further is that a child needs three square (balanced) meals a day. In reality children do not need three balanced meals a day, or even three meals a day for that matter. Most of us have followed this plan without any thought to whether the child is hungry at the scheduled time or what foods the child is craving.

Here we might mention the particular fetish that has developed about breakfast. We are told that you must have a good breakfast to get a start on the day, that breakfast is the most important meal of the day, and that for perennial weight watchers, eating a good breakfast will assist in keeping one's weight down. But not everyone likes or wants breakfast. One mother said it made her "crazy" that her nine-year-old daughter did not want breakfast, and every morning began with an unpleasant argument between them. Although her daughter consistently stated she was not hungry in the morning, her mother was locked into the breakfast myth. Furthermore, she felt that providing her daughter with this meal meant she was a "good mother." Not only was her daughter breaking with convention, but she was also interfering in her mother's valued way of beginning the day and providing good parenting. This mother had not thought of the possibility of sending her daughter off to school with a "breakfast" snack—crackers and cheese, apple slices or a peanut butter and jelly sandwich—which she could eat as her hunger dictated. This alternative might not have been the "ideal" breakfast, but it would have met her child's physical hunger and saved everybody from the morning fray.

Still another variation on the "proper meal" theme is the idea that good equals hot. There is a full range of nutritious foods that don't have to be served hot. Children sometimes prefer cold or raw foods that are readily available and easily prepared. Nutritionists point out that food values are often greater when vitamins aren't cooked away.

When, at our workshops, we first suggest to parents that the "balanced meal" or the three-meal-a-day concept be abandoned, the clamor in the room is often deafening. Parents will cry out, "You're not suggesting that I send Norman to school without a solid breakfast under his belt?" Or, "You don't mean to say that Sally should go to bed without having had a proper dinner?" Indeed, we *are* saying if Norman isn't hungry in the morning, he need not eat breakfast. If dinnertime does not coincide with Sally's hunger, then that is not when she should eat. We expect you to meet these ideas with a skeptical eye. They are not the conventional wisdom, but we believe you can provide the necessary foods for healthy growth and development by responding to your child's hunger whenever it arises. This can be done in a way that creates pleasure for the child and less tension and work for you.

Myth: The Clean Plate Is a Worthy Goal

Four-year-old Johnny is served his dinner, but is dawdling and picking at his food. His parents are worried that he isn't eating enough, and father tries a time-honored ploy: "Let's see who is going to be in the Clean Plate Club tonight."

For those of you who didn't grow up with a Clean Plate Club, you earn membership by eating *everything* on your plate. The rewards vary. In some families the reward is simply a calm meal because child and parents are not struggling over how little spinach or broccoli is eaten. In other families actual rewards are given, an extra half hour of TV, a small present or a promise of a special dessert, such as ice cream or candy. We were told that in one family the reward was being allowed to wear father's World War II army medals for the rest of the evening. With these medals pinned to the child's blouse, she walked around looking like a little general. The trouble is that she did not have command over her own inner terrain.

Children have always devised ways to get those plates clean —one way or another. Many a pet has given up pet food for the more delicious morsels passed under the table. One parent remembered hiding his food behind the radiator as a child.

Another bribed her younger brother to eat her food while their parents' backs were turned. Mouthfuls and napkins full of food have been secretly held by children impatient for the evening meal to end. In one family, the children, eager to please, licked their plates and announced that the plates were "*so clean* they don't have to be washed."

The message of the Clean Plate Club is that there will be an *external* reward for eating. Eating is not connected to feeding physical hunger. It may be dictated by the parents' sense of how much is enough for the child's growing needs. It is also frequently about a demand for respect for the parents' labor in the kitchen. We understand that it is difficult for parents to see the food that they have painstakingly prepared not eaten. However, having to clean her plate interferes with the child's self-control in eating. The child may feel accepted, but the price of acceptance is high. She is stuffed and uncomfortable at the end of the meal. And, more important, her natural feelings of fullness are invalidated. She is in effect being taught that fullness has to do with what mommy or daddy say—not what her tummy tells her.

Adults who grew up in Clean Plate Club families tell us that they continue to eat the food that is served to them rather than listen to their bodily sensations of hunger and satiation. What you want and need are not necessarily determined by the amount of food on your plate. The clean-plate lesson is difficult to unlearn.

Other Feeding Ploys

Mike's father wants him to eat more. In order to encourage Mike to finish his dinner, he uses a number of common feeding techniques. He tells his son to "take a bite for Grandma." When that bite is swallowed, Mike is urged to take one for Uncle Bill. Bites are then taken for Momma, Poppa, Sister and the rest of the O'Connor clan. If Mike takes the bite for Grandma, he is rewarded with praise and feels acceptance from both Father, who is feeding him, and Grandma. If he does not take this bite, he feels he is doing something against Father and Grandma. What is communicated is that eating can be *for* someone else or *against* someone else, but not that it is *for oneself.*

Some of you may remember food on a spoon being waved around in front of you with a *choo-choo* sound because now it was a train going into a tunnel or with a *whoosh-zoom* sound because it was an airplane going into a hangar. These games can be fun for parent and child, but it is important that both parent and child understand that the tunnel or hangar can close down at the *child's* request. Then, the game allows for physical hunger to be met and for the child to determine what and how much she eats.

Many feeding tricks involve threats and promises. "If you don't drink your milk, you will get sick." "If you eat carrots, your eyesight will improve." One parent remembered being told that if she ate carrots, they would make her pretty. She said she spent hours eating carrots and glancing in the mirror eagerly waiting for major changes to take place. While it is all right to teach your children good nutrition, this shouldn't be used to manipulate what the child herself wants to eat. A most popular and baffling parental line handed to children is the one that encourages them to eat because children elsewhere are starving. Depending on your generation, you may have heard this as, "Eat what's on your plate because children are starving in Europe"; if you are a little younger, you may have eaten because of starvation in China, India or Africa. This bit of nonsense was well responded to by the child who suggested, "Let's put my peas in an envelope and mail them off to all those hungry kids."

Other children have taken this caution very seriously and have felt guilty for rejecting or perhaps wasting food when children elsewhere are in great need. The child is subtly being told he is ungrateful. The underlying threat suggests that he too may end up starved—of approval, attention and maybe even food (being sent off to bed without dinner) if he doesn't finish what's on his plate.

Leaving Tradition Behind

When our children were infants, most of us fed them on demand. We trusted that they knew when and how much to eat. As they grew, we imposed a structure on their eating behavior as well as numerous rules we believed were necessary either for nutritional reasons, for preserving family harmony or otherwise for the best interest of the child. Unfortunately, few of us stopped to examine whether it was really necessary to interfere so much with our children's natural eating instincts.

The fact is that children, from infancy to adulthood, are capable of regulating their own eating. Their best interests will be served when we can abandon the myths, the games, the ploys and the scare tactics that teach our children to disregard their internal cues and to eat according to outside formulas.

There are very few areas where young children can exercise control over their lives. Parents decide what the child's environment will be, what she will wear, how she will be taught. They make endless other decisions about the child's life. By allowing the child to decide when to eat, what to eat, and how much to eat, we can strengthen her self-confidence, self-esteem and sense of dignity and also avoid the kinds of eating difficulties that have plagued many of us for life.

3

SELF–DEMAND FEEDING

It's important to remember that children have a remarkable inborn mechanism that lets them know how much food and which types of food they need for normal growth and development. It is extremely rare to see serious malnutrition or vitamin deficiency or infectious disease result from a feeding problem. . . . The aim is not to make the child eat but to let her natural appetite come to the surface so that she wants to eat.

Dr. Benjamin Spock,
BABY AND CHILD CARE

Imagine this: You are a child being raised by parents who respect the fact that you must learn to have control over your own body. They take their cues from you. They look for the signs that indicate hunger and differentiate those hunger cues from other urges and needs you may have. When you are an infant, your mother allows you to drink as much as you need and knows that you will stop when full. As you get older and solid foods are introduced, your parents attempt to time the offering of the new foods to your signals of hunger. They learn which foods you like and dislike, and they notice how your tastes change. They do not stick to a rigid schedule of feeding, even though they see certain patterns emerging in your eating habits. They are flexible enough to allow for variations in terms of food choices, time of feedings and amounts. This way of handling your early experiences with food and eating continues throughout your childhood and adolescence. It leads, eventually, to a well-developed ability to tune into your own cues of physiological hunger, to determine exactly which food will fill that hunger, and to stop eating when full.

Does all this sound idyllic? Impossible to achieve? Unrealistic? The hypothetical parents in this account are simply following an approach we call self-demand feeding. Self-demand feeding means responding to a child's physiological hunger with food and allowing the child to be self-directed. Paradoxical as it may sound, granting freedom in the world of food allows the child to develop inner control.

For most of us, hunger and questions about hunger have been obscured. If you are an adult seeing a doctor for a weight problem, you're likely to emerge from your visit with a printed diet in your hand. It would be unusual for the physician to explore the issue of hunger—how to recognize it, how to wait for it, what to feed it. Similarly, if you take your child to a pediatrician for either excessive weight gain or unwillingness to eat, the doctor is unlikely to discuss hunger as a key issue.

When we gave a talk on self-demand feeding to doctors from a major teaching hospital in New York City, one physician stood up and asked his colleagues, "How many of us ask our patients with weight and eating problems if they know what hunger is?" Not one hand was raised.

At a conference for people in the field of nutrition education, the keynote speaker was sharing results of her study of children and eating patterns. She was reporting how children learned about food choices and how they developed their eating habits. Not once in this study was a child asked if s/he ate with hunger. It never occurred to this researcher to ask this question.

Hunger is the key to eating. There is no other good reason to eat. Yet, many of us eat when we're not hungry. We eat because it is *time* to eat. We eat because we planned to eat at six o'clock and the food is ready. We eat because we are afraid if we don't eat now, there won't be anything later. We eat because it is polite to do so when we're offered food in a social situation. We eat so as not to offend others. We eat because the food tastes good, though we might enjoy it even better if we ate it when we're hungry.

There are also emotional reasons for turning to food. Many of us reach for food when we're anxious and need soothing; when we are lonely and need company; to distract us from feelings of anger, depression, neediness, ambivalence, sexual longing . . . Since we ourselves eat for so many reasons having nothing to do with *physical hunger,* it is little wonder that we pass along to our children confused messages about eating.

We have come a long way from the days when force-feeding infants was a common practice. Most people know that it is unwise to put a newborn on a schedule of feedings every four hours. The new mother is instructed in the *wisdom* of demand feeding. She is told that her infant knows when she is hungry, knows how much she needs to fill that hunger and even knows when to stop.

Unfortunately, the demand feeding that we encourage for infants goes by the wayside as the child grows older. We somehow forget what we learned about the body being self-regulatory. Although we know that hunger makes itself felt, we stop allowing our children's natural feelings to determine when and what they will be fed. Pediatricians concluded long ago that four-hour feedings should be done away with because babies could thrive better on their own schedules. Why, then, do we begin to impose schedules while our children are still so young?

Parents believe that when solid foods are introduced, there will be less work for everyone if the child can sit at the dinner table and eat the same food as the rest of the family. However, the battles over the child's not wanting to eat, or wanting to eat earlier or later, or wanting a different food than the one prepared, turn out to take more time and energy than anyone bargained for. Letting children eat with physiological hunger, whenever it may occur, and giving children the foods of their choice in the long run does not create more work for parents. As we'll describe, using self-demand feeding will result in less work for parents and certainly less irritation.

As parents, we know that our job is to teach our children how to eat properly. We must teach them how to sit at a table and how to handle first a spoon and eventually a fork and knife. As they grow, we teach them table manners and how to choose nutritious and well-balanced foods. Unfortunately, part of this socialization has included imposing rules on eating behavior that injure the child's natural ability to eat with hunger. Thus, we teach our children to eat three times a day, when in fact their hunger might lead them to eat in smaller quantities four, six or eight times a day. The three-meal-a-day rule is one of several that disregard the child's natural internal time clock and discourage her from relying on her own hunger cues.

The rules regarding food choices have the same undesirable effect. We have uncritically accepted the convention that each meal has a specific set of food choices. Breakfast is a time for cereal, toast, juice, and eggs. Lunch is a time for a sandwich, soup or a salad. And at dinner meat or fish, vegetables, potatoes, and dessert must be served. Heaven forbid that a child should feel like eating lamb chops for breakfast or pancakes for dinner. Such a choice is unacceptable.

Even within each meal the order of the courses is fixed by tradition. Soup is always first and dessert always last. Can you imagine serving your child dessert first? These conventions leave no room for the child to eat in response to her natural desires.

Ten-year-old Mary sits down to dinner and says she only wants the baked potato with lots of butter. Her mother says that she can skip the soup if she wants to, but she can't just eat a baked potato without having some steak or peas. Mary wants to know why. Her mother explains that it's not done that way and "you have to have your protein. Take a little bit of everything on your plate," she says, "and at least taste each item." Mary still insists that she only wants the baked potato.

Mary's mother means well. She wants Mary to go out into the world and be "normal" and "healthy." To most mothers, this means eating "well-balanced, nutritious" meals. Being normal also means that when you eat dinner, you eat a bit of everything served. It is considered nutritionally unsound to allow a child to have only potatoes for dinner, but Mary's craving is a signal of what her body needs. She can be forced to eat the rest of the meal, but each time that happens, she becomes less able to recognize and trust her own body's cues.

In 1928, Dr. Clara Davis did a groundbreaking study of children's eating behavior in a controlled environment. She exposed children to a full range of foods and then observed that when left to their own devices, they chose a well-balanced diet. Her findings suggest that while Mary might choose a potato today, tomorrow she will want salad or meat or other foods that will balance her diet. Over a relatively short period of time she will vary her intake and eat what her body needs. Her hunger will guide her.

We saw a good example of this when Allen and Kathy came for a consultation. They were at their wits end over three-year-old Nicky's eating behavior. Nicky was making dinner an impossible and dreaded event in their household. Like many of us, Allen and Kathy felt that dinner was a time for family members to come together at the end of a day. Eating what was served at the table was part of that event. As Kathy described her family's problem, "Every night at six o'clock we all sit down to eat. Nicky usually doesn't want what I've made or he insists on only one item. I try to coax him along by saying, 'Let me just put the spaghetti on your plate along with the hamburger, and you can try it if you want.' He gets very angry at me, shoves the plate away and refuses to eat. I finally relent and give him just the hamburger. At this point he asks, 'What is that white stuff in my hamburger?' I say, 'Onions.' Then he refuses to eat it because he says he doesn't want 'white' in his hamburgers. It's enough to drive you crazy. Then he turns to his father and asks, 'When can I have dessert?' We explain that dessert comes after you've eaten dinner. He begins to pick at the salad and after each bite asks, 'Now can I have dessert?' or 'How many bites must I eat before I can get dessert?' And this", she said, "is just the dinnertime problem!"

"At the day care center, Nicky's eating is no different. The center feels the same way we do, that you eat what's put in front of you. The children cook lunch together and eat what they have prepared. They make nutritious meals, but Nicky finds fault. One day he won't eat because he doesn't like the color of the soup being served. Another day it is the smell of the meat. As a matter of fact, for most of the year Nicky has eaten little or none of the food served for lunch at the day care center. Because he comes home hungry at the end of the day,

I give him a little snack to tide him over until we sit down to dinner together."

Nicky is not unusual. Many children who refuse food are struggling to be self-regulating. They want to choose their own foods and eat when they are hungry. At first, this may be at odds with the family's structured eating plan. We urged Kathy and Allen to give up the controls and let Nicky have exactly what he wanted even if it was strange to everyone else. That would mean he could eat hamburger and nothing else at dinner. They could send him to school with foods he liked, including breakfast foods, which, in fact, he was fond of and ate without complaint every morning. Then at lunch if he didn't want to eat the day care center's food, he would have another choice. In a few weeks Kathy called to say how relieved the whole family was. There was much less tension around food, and, in fact, their son was eating quite normally. He might not eat a fully balanced diet at each meal, but over a few days he ate a wide range of foods, including all the basic nutritional elements.

Small children can take a liking to a particular food and want it every day for a week or more and then switch to another food. This is quite normal. One five-year-old stopped eating, and when his mother asked him why, he replied, "Dodo [his imaginary friend] has run away from home because he doesn't like your cooking." The mother pursued the conversation and asked, "What does Dodo want to eat?" and Bobby said, "Dodo wants peanut butter sandwiches."

The mother told Bobby to explain to Dodo that he could have all the peanut butter sandwiches he wanted. Dodo returned and Bobby began to eat peanut butter sandwiches a few times a day, along with some other foods. This mother was able to tune into her son's needs and desires in a very caring and creative way. His food demand did not become a big issue, and within a short period of time Bobby's peanut butter passion was down to modest proportions.

One four-year-old took a liking to ice cream for a week. Every time she was hungry, she asked for ice cream, and it was given to her. She ate it at least three times a day. A few weeks later there was a run on breakfast cereals, and after that it was broccoli.

Confronted with the idea of allowing children to eat like

this, most parents will ask, "What about nutrition and the need for a balanced diet?" As we discussed in chapter two, if a child has no particular health problem, she should be allowed to experiment with different foods, and no fuss should be made over the interest in or desire for any particular food. Ice cream should be treated like broccoli, fish, yogurt, or any other food your child may want to eat. If you make ice cream a "special" food, you are saying something about these other foods. You have never heard a parent say, "If you finish your cake, you can have some broccoli." The child learns that certain foods are a must, even if they aren't so good to eat. Ice cream is the real treat that can be eaten only after you get through the musts. No surprise, then, that ice cream is what the child wants because she knows that she can't always have it.

Children can learn to trust their own hunger signals and then make a choice of what to eat based on *what their bodies need at that moment.* When no food is more special than any other, the child can meet her specific hunger, that is, eat the "just-right food." Foods do have different nutritional values, but if sweets—in a psychological sense—are equal to vegetables, then a hungry child has the possibility of choosing one over the other based solely on what her body is calling for.

"Legalizing" foods—allowing your child to have *as much* or *as little* as she wants of a particular food—is an essential ingredient to the self-demand feeding approach. If you limit your child's access to and intake of a particular food—candy bars, cookies, soda—it is just those foods that your child will want desperately. The forbidden food will shine in neon lights as if it were playing on Broadway. But if you legalize it, she will turn to the special food at first and then, in a relatively short time, take little interest in it. You may think this sounds unlikely but two recent incidents, among many others, demonstrate the point:

"A struggle developed in my family over chocolate kisses. The children would insist on my buying some each time I went shopping. They would consume the kisses in twenty minutes and then pester me for more. After weeks of this battle—my saying 'No, you can't have so many,' or doling them out in small quantities and hearing endless choruses of 'Ma, I want more' —I finally applied the self-demand-feeding approach. On my next trip to the supermarket I bought each child four family-sized packs of kisses. This supply was greater than the amount they could eat in one sitting. I told them that when the supply was half gone, they should let me know and I would replenish it. They would never have to worry again about running out of kisses. I didn't hear about kisses until weeks later when their playmates were visiting and ate through the supply. At that time I was asked to buy more. Up to that point I saw unopened chocolate kisses around the apartment and squirreled away in various jacket and pants pockets and assorted hideouts. Not all that many were eaten. By legalizing the kisses and giving them in great supply, what I was really saying was that chocolate kisses are fine, here they are for you, they will never be forbidden, and as a matter of fact, it is up to you to decide from *inside yourself* when you want them and how many you really want."

Nancy, mother of eight-year-old Julie, came for a consultation. Julie was overweight and showed signs of compulsive eating. In taking background information we learned that when Julie was an infant, she had been labeled "slow to thrive." She had lost a considerable amount of weight after she came home from the hospital. She failed by far to meet the popular expectation that infants will double their birth weight within the first four or five months of life. Nancy had had trouble breast feeding; her milk wasn't rich enough, the supply was low, and she felt under great pressure to get Julie to eat. Breast feeding was supplemented with bottles, and there was great joy in Julie's weight gain. Her eating was treated as a "big deal" by the family. They applauded every swallow and later every bite of food. As she grew to be a toddler, Julie learned to please mommy and daddy by eating as much as possible. The only problem was that she never learned about hunger.

When she realized that Julie had developed a problem with overeating, Nancy suddenly began restricting food intake. She told Julie there were foods she could eat in quantity—most vegetables, for example—and foods that she had to limit— sweets and carbohydrates. Naturally, the child wanted the restricted foods. Mealtimes were particularly awful, although the war raged throughout the day. When Nancy came for help, we advised her to take away the power food had assumed by lifting the food bans and giving the controls back to Julie. Julie's eating had been subject to so much manipulation that food now meant many things to her that had nothing to do with satisfaction of hunger. At first, Julie might not believe that she was really being given free reign to choose what and how much to eat. She would test this freedom to the limit and possibly, at the beginning, gain some weight under this approach.

Nancy told Julie that she was the one who was best equipped to know when she was hungry and for which foods. Julie, who obviously didn't believe a word of this, immediately asked for crackers, and Nancy handed Julie the *box of crackers* instead of the usual daily allotment of two. Julie made a substantial dent in the supply waiting for someone to stop her. When no one did, she carried the box around for half an hour, but didn't eat any more that day.

A few hours later Julie asked for raisins. Her mother handed her eight small boxes. Julie ate through six of them. Each day Julie asked for foods that previously had been restricted, such as ice cream, pasta, donuts, certain cheeses, breads . . . Each food request was met with an abundant supply.

The next few months were a test for everyone. Julie wanted potato chips one morning at breakfast. The next day at breakfast she asked for a full bowl of cereal, eggs, toast with peanut butter, more crackers and juice. She was given everything she wanted, though she only ate a part of it.

In six months time Nancy reported that there was no longer a struggle over Julie's eating. Indeed, Nancy felt relieved of the burden of having to monitor and carefully dole out food to her daughter. She no longer felt like a "supply sergeant," and Julie was just as pleased to be rid of the conflict. Julie's weight stabilized at first. After a year of self-demand feeding, she grew normally in height and lost some weight, with the net effect that she no longer was an overweight child. Julie now has the chance of growing up recognizing her hunger and knowing how to feed it.

The idea that a child can choose when to eat, what to eat, and how much to eat may sound revolutionary. Yet we have seen over and over again that the approach that works well with an infant can be applied to an older child as well. This does not mean anarchy, a "Chaotic Kitchen," or a "Dictatorship of the Children"! Many parents may hear self-demand feeding as their enslavement. To the contrary, feeding on demand can liberate parents from kitchen routines and dining room struggles. Essentially you need only have a variety of foods available—not all cooked or hot—and allow the child to choose from these when hungry. The selection doesn't have to be enormous. There should be a reasonable variety of foods consistent with the family's style of living and its budget. Parents may decide to cook upon request, but having cooked, they don't have to do additional food preparation if the child changes her mind. (See chapter four, "When, What and How Much.")

You are probably wondering what will happen under this approach to the traditional "mealtime," that most sacred family gathering. Think back to your own childhood for a moment. Did you look forward to dinner every night or do you remember times when it was an uncomfortable experience to get through? For many families dinnertime is filled with tension. Dad and Mom are exhausted after a day at work. The children are starved because they have waited too long to eat or else they have snacked before dinner and don't want to eat. Also, anxiety can build over food preferences that have been indulged or disregarded, the amounts of food eaten or not eaten, proper table manners, the attention given to each family member, as well as various discipline or other family issues.

Wouldn't it be better if everyone ate when they were hungry and instead of sharing *food* together, family members shared *time* together? For example, you could set 7:00 P.M. as family hour. At seven the whole family would come together. Perhaps the gathering would be held in the kitchen or dining room, and those who were hungry would eat. Others could join in and share the events of the day without eating. The tension of having to eat would be removed. Younger children might have eaten at five and perhaps will snack again at seven with the rest of the family before they go to bed. Older children might eat with the parents at seven or later. The parents may want a drink at this gathering and decide to eat alone after the family hour is over. There would be no pressure to eat at this specific time. Food would be available, and people would *eat according to hunger, independent of the social situation.*

4

WHEN, WHAT AND HOW MUCH

We try to give the children the conviction that food is always amply available, and the best way to do that is to be ready to produce it at any time of the day or the night. It is in this sense that all times are mealtimes, though this does not lessen, but rather increases the importance of the main meals. With the children eating off and on during the day, they never get so hungry that they cannot afford to be social at table; thus there is no need to concentrate on the fare to the exclusion of the personal interchange that goes on at table.

Bruno Bettelheim,
LOVE IS NOT ENOUGH

You may be saying to yourself, "Okay, it all sounds interesting, but how do we switch over to such a different way of feeding our children?" Here is a step-by-step guide to help you. It all revolves around three simple questions: Are you hungry? What do you want to eat? Are you full?

Step One:
Are You Hungry?

Start by telling your children that from now on they will be in control of their eating. Do this in whatever language is appropriate to the age of your child. Let it be clear that whenever they are hungry, they can choose foods they like from what is available in the house. Each time they ask for food, you will simply ask, "Are you hungry?" This question is crucial and should be asked routinely, even if you begin to feel like a broken record. From early childhood, even before your child can talk herself, begin to ask, "Does your tummy feel empty or hungry?" The goal is to communicate and reinforce a simple but important message: Requests for food should be made when—and only when—there is a feeling of hunger.

One parent of a three-year-old, who started with step one, reported, "I asked Gina if she was hungry whenever she approached me with a food request. I felt a bit idiotic repeating the question so often. And each time I asked, she would automatically say yes, and of course I would give her the food. After two weeks, one evening at bedtime she asked me, 'Mama, what does *hungry* mean?' It was only then that I explained to her, for the first time, that *hunger* meant an empty feeling in her belly that would go away if she ate." Though slightly belated, this was an important beginning lesson for Gina about hunger and its relationship to food.

Your child may answer yes to the question "Are you hungry?" without really knowing yet what hunger is. That is fine for now. You should give her food each time she asks for it, whether or not it is clear that she is hungry. In the beginning it is important to offer food each time the request is made. The requests will get hooked up with hunger eventually. Even if she says, "No, I'm not hungry," but wants food anyway, be sure you do not withhold the food. You will notice that the requests will diminish when the child is *certain* that food will always be there for her. Once food availability is established, it will be easier to figure out that sometimes when she asks for food and is clearly not physically hungry, she may be "hungry" for something else.

Ten-year-old Jim came into the kitchen after dinner one night wanting something to eat. His mother, who had just introduced the self-demand feeding approach, asked if Jim was hungry. Jim said no and his mother turned the conversation to how the homework was going. A child may be bored or confused about homework or may just want a break and some human contact and interaction. Separating the food question from other issues, the family can begin to deal with the latter appropriately.

Sometimes it can be difficult to know if your child is hungry or needs attention. One way to find this out is to give her alternatives to choose from: "Jane, do you want to eat now or would you rather we read a book together or play a game of checkers?" If she is hungry, she will choose the food. If she's not, you've given her the chance to let you know what is on her mind.

It may take time for you as well as for your child to be able to tell accurately when he is physiologically hungry. If your child is used to eating because *it is time to eat,* getting him to ignore the clock and connect eating with hunger will take some work. You will have to begin by letting him know that he is no longer restricted to eating at mealtimes but can eat whenever his stomach feels hungry. (As we discussed earlier, if mealtimes are important to you as a gathering point in the day, they can be preserved as a family time, even if not everyone eats at that moment.) Basically you will be encouraging your child to relearn what he knew as an infant—to recognize the feeling and to eat when hunger is felt.

If certain foods have been restricted that are now being allowed, parents can expect some testing behavior. The child may eat more of the restricted foods than hunger dictates out of fear that they may not be there in the future. When Jamie, age nine, first started on self-demand feeding, he asked for pretzels constantly and ate quantities that clearly exceeded his needs. Finally, his mother gave him a huge supply and watched Jamie go at it. Despite her worry that this binge would never end, Jamie's mother stuck to her guns and replenished the supply whenever it was half gone, never allowing it to dwindle to nothing. The testing lasted for several days before Jamie's interest in pretzels diminished. By that time Jamie was convinced that his mother was not going to reimpose a limit and that he really was being allowed to control his own pretzel intake. When he was no longer afraid that the food would disappear Jamie did not eat pretzels past the point of hunger.

Sometimes children don't eat when they are hungry. This often happens when they are preoccupied with what they are doing. For example, if a child is afraid she will miss out on some other activity—seeing a TV program, playing some special game or sport—she may not stop to eat. If possible, she should be encouraged to take a break when she is hungry, eat something and return to the activity. This may seem disruptive, but it will help your child become tuned in to her own body signals and the need to respond to them. Just as you would encourage a child to stop playing to use the bathroom if she needs to, you may have to remind her to respond to her hunger cues when they arise.

Children may deny their hunger when they have been taught by their parents that eating in some particular circumstance is forbidden. If your child has received a firm message that she should not eat between meals, at ballet class, or on the street, then the natural feelings of hunger may get suppressed. We encourage, to the extent possible, that food be available at all times. You can carry crackers or quartered sandwiches or nuts and raisins. When children know the food is there and that they can respond to their hunger *when* they feel it, they become quite tuned in to these bodily cues. You may expect that when your child does begin to recognize hunger signs and to feed herself when hunger arises, she will eat frequently during the day in small quantities rather than larger quantities a few times a day.

A problem we all face, children and adults alike, is the temptation to eat special foods (that is, those *not* generally available) even when we aren't hungry. Who can resist a real delicacy—whether it's steak, lobster or a favorite dessert when it is offered? Sometimes it's simply impossible to apply the "hunger test" strictly. A slight modification might be to ask your child if he is hungry and, if he's not, to tell him he can take a little taste of the special food now and save the rest for later when he is hungry. One family wraps and marks the special food with the child's initials, thereby sealing the promise that it will be there when he's hungry. And, of course, the food will be all the more enjoyable when eaten with appetite.

The important lesson is that as few obstacles as possible

should be placed in the way of the child's learning to feel and respond to his hunger. There will naturally be some occasions for you and your child when this doesn't work out, but they don't have to worry you. Even with occasional slips, the object remains to transform eating behavior so that food is eaten only when hunger calls.

Step Two:
What Do You Want to Eat?

Ask your child *what* she wants to eat. At first she will probably request foods that she thinks you will not approve of. Be prepared! This testing will continue until the child is sure you are not going to withhold certain foods. Before you ask the question, "What would you like to eat?" try to anticipate the probable range of responses. Since you know your child's food tastes, be sure the items that she likes are on hand so that when the request comes, it can be met without a lot of trouble.

Keep in mind that hunger has two aspects. There is, first, the feeling of an emptiness inside. Second, you need to identify exactly what kind of food will most satisfyingly meet the hunger pang: the *specific hunger*. Your child must learn to make that match. Determining what food you really want is called reading your hunger. No matter how much you love chocolate, you know that hunger for soup or meat and potatoes will not be satisfied by a Hershey bar. We have found that much over-eating is caused by people's failure to read their hunger properly. When you do that accurately and make the proper food match, you will feel satisfied. No amount of consumption of the wrong foods—for example, sweets when pasta is desired—will bring satisfaction. Your child will eat proper amounts of food if she is fed what her hunger craves.

To help the youngster decide what food he's hungry for, ask him if it's something hot or something cold. This begins to narrow the field. You might try to determine if he's needing a protein, carbohydrate or fruit or vegetable—is it meat, a sandwich, a fruit salad? You can refine this inquiry further by asking him to think about whether the food he desires is spicy, mild, chewy, crunchy, smooth, sweet, sour, or salty. Foods have different tastes, textures, smells and consistencies. Run through the list of what's available in the house, and once a choice is made, explore with him if it's really on target. With a young child you can try this: Have him imagine the food going down to his stomach. He should pretend that he's taking a bite of it. Does it feel right in his belly? If not, what would be a better match? An eight-year-old learning to read his hunger said, "I want something hot and cheesy. A cheese omelet? No, not right. Crunchy too. I know—melted cheese on toast." With time children can become quite adept at reading their hunger.

With an eleven- or twelve-year-old, you can raise the level of the questions but still concentrate on trying to pinpoint the specific food that would feel good now.

It is critical to this process that all foods be "legalized" and "equalized." Initially, parents have to come to terms with their own fear of foods. Forbidden foods, those we do not allow into the home or that we label as bad, are precisely the ones that both parent and child want in excess. It is their forbidden quality that make them so attractive.

At a workshop we gave, one mother said, "Does that mean when my son says, 'I'm hungry,' and asks for gumdrops, I should give him gumdrops? That's all he will ever eat!" Her fear that he would eat only gumdrops seems to stem from her belief that she herself would be unable to stop devouring gumdrops. To protect herself, she did not allow gumdrops in the house. Yet we've seen that when gumdrops are treated like celery, they are not eaten in excess by parents *or* their children.

We asked this mother to try an experiment: To remove the "forbidden" label attached to gumdrops, she would give them to her son *in excess* each time he said he was hungry for them. She was to make sure a supply was always available and that he knew it was there. Three weeks later this mother reported that the plan had worked. Her son lost his intense interest in gumdrops once they became just another food on the shelf. He ate them occasionally but not to the extent that she feared. She also found that with so many gumdrops around, she herself had less desire for them and felt less afraid of them.

We have seen over and over again that children will, in fact, select a wide variety of foods when they are available and when special and symbolic attachments are reduced to a minimum. When eating is not a matter of intrigue or reward, children make healthy selections. On self-demand feeding, they choose meats, fish, cheese, vegetables and fruits as well as sweets.

When children say they are hungry and ask only for sweets, you could respond, "You can have the cookies if you want them, but we also have cereal, tuna, yogurt, peanut butter and fruit in the house. Maybe you would like one of those things. Or, maybe you want to start with a cookie and then have some tuna or peanut butter." It is quite common for children to change their minds or to start with the cookie and then switch to the other food. They may even hold the cookie while they wait for or even eat the alternative food. They feel secure that their food choice has been validated and that their cookie will be there when it is wanted.

Sometimes a child will tell a parent what she wants to eat and the parent will try to discourage her. Esther, the mother of nine-year-old Fran, said, "The other night we went out for dinner, and Fran wanted chicken pot pie. I found myself telling her all the reasons she wouldn't like chicken pot pie. I told her it had peas in it and crust all around. As she continued to insist on the chicken pot pie, I kept reeling off reasons why I knew she wouldn't like it. Finally, I asked myself why I was doing this and realized how controlling I was being about her food choice. She got the chicken pot pie and proceeded to eat all of it except for a few peas." Parents sometimes don't realize how much they interfere with their child's food selections. As you are encouraging your child to develop a greater sensitivity to her specific hunger, you should not confuse her likes and dislikes with your own.

You may be wondering whether you can respond to your family's food choices without constantly running out to the store. No one wants to do that, nor can the person who does the shopping be expected to be a mind reader about what others may want to eat. Keep a piece of paper, a shopping list, tacked to the refrigerator door or someplace else your children can reach. Then all members of the family can write down what they would like the next time the shopping is done. This shopping list puts the responsibility on each individual for making decisions about (a) what it is s/he wants; and (b) what supplies of his/hers may be running low. A younger child who cannot write should be asked before the list leaves the house, "What would you like from the store?"

A child usually knows what she wants and can be very specific, so that a list might include strawberry yogurt, Swiss cheese, coffee ice cream, raisins and chicken. Not only will the list be specific as to flavors, it may also be specific as to brands —not all chocolate chip cookies taste the same. Participating in the food selection helps the child learn the choices that are available. Naturally, you will need to put limits on the number of choices made to fit within your budget. The family budget is a normal constraint of life, which children can understand. But take care that the limit setting not be done in a punitive way or in a way that tells the child you really won't let her make choices. Once the message of variety and choice has been communicated, you'll be surprised at how easy and predictable it all becomes.

Step Three:
Are You Full?

This question helps the child learn that after hunger is matched with a food of his choosing, eating can stop when he is *full*. In order to learn when to stop, the child has to feel assured that there is more than enough for him. If there is an ample supply, he will have to determine *from inside* when to stop.

For example, if your son likes potato chips, there should be more bags of potato chips than he can eat at one time. Perhaps four bags would be right for a start. He will have to look at that sea of potato chips and really decide from the vantage point of plentitude how much will be enough. It will no longer be possible simply to eat until it's all gone. Nor will it be necessary to gobble up whatever he can in order to ensure getting his share. Of course, supplies must be replenished when they are getting low so that the child does not select a food because he is fearful that there won't be more later.

To get this idea across, we suggest giving each child a shelf or an area where he can keep those specific foods that are important to him. You may decide to give him a vegetable bin in the refrigerator and/or a shelf in a pantry or a large plastic container with his name on it. These "shelf" foods will change as his food tastes change: One week it may be animal cookies and yogurt; another week peanut butter and grapes. In addition to individual shelves, there will probably be a general staple food supply from which all family members can choose. If many members of the family like the same foods, it is important to buy enough so that people are not competing for fear that someone else will eat all of these foods.

Part of the importance of establishing each child's own shelf is that ownership of foods on that shelf is inviolate. No one but the shelf owner is allowed to take food from it. Thus, each child's "special" foods are reserved for her, and adequate supplies are guaranteed. You should remind your child that there is plenty of food, and if she is full now, she can save some special food for when she gets hungry later.

In step one, you were helping your child to assess her own hunger from inside. Now you are trying to get her to learn that she can tell all by herself when she has had enough to eat. Make sure that you introduce this idea of fullness in a way that doesn't make the child feel you are questioning her selection or amounts. If you feel disgusted by her food choice or the amount she is consuming, then this is not the time to say with a smile on your face, "Aren't you full yet, darling?" Children know perfectly well when we are trying to control them and when we are feeling displeased.

Too often fullness is determined by external cues. A very common cue is allowing what is on the plate to determine fullness. For a child this means that the portion served is supposed to match her hunger. This isn't necessarily so. The parent must be willing to provide second portions and be willing to wrap or throw away uneaten food. Until she learns how to tell when she's full, the child's request for a particular portion of food may be more or less than she actually needs to fill her hunger. The message should always be: Eat until you are full.

In our fast-paced and time-oriented world children's ability to tell when they're full is often interfered with by time constraints. If a child gets twenty-five minutes to eat lunch in school and is a slow eater, his eating may be stopped by the bell at the end of the lunch period rather than by a feeling of fullness. At home a child's ability to finish what he's eating in time to go on the family outing may dictate how much he gets to eat. It's hard to control the amount of time allotted to lunch at school but, whenever possible, the clock shouldn't dictate how much a child will eat. A feeling of satisfaction in his stomach should be the only reason his eating stops.

Since children learn through imitation and because they want to do things that mommy and daddy or older siblings do, they may judge their own fullness by when other people seem full. Of course, each family member is different and will reach fullness at a different time. Individual differences should be encouraged as well as respected.

One mother described the process in her house: "One night my three-year-old daughter told me she wanted applesauce and meat, but she wanted to start with vanilla ice cream. I looked at her and said, 'How can you eat all that?' She explained, 'I have a lot of rooms in my tummy,' and then pointed to spots on her stomach where each food would go. She *did* eat all three items in the order she chose until she filled up her little rooms."

5

PARENTS ASK . . .

Does This Mean
I Must Cook All Day Long?

The answer to this common concern is an emphatic NO! Here
are some suggestions for handling the situation: Decide what
meal you will prepare that evening—or day—if any. You can
take inventory to see if anyone is hungry for that meal. If
no one is hungry, you can decide (a) not to cook; (b) to
cook for yourself; or (c) to cook the meal and save it for
later.

You can prepare food and put it aside so that your child
will be able to help herself when a feeling of hunger arises—
unless, of course, she is very young and needs help. If you
decide to cook only for yourself, other family members can
choose to eat from among available foods that do not require
preparation—or need only minor preparation—such as sandwiches, fruits, cheeses, cereals and so forth. Making a cold
meal is relatively simple and does not require a lot of
cleaning up afterward. What is not eaten can be covered
and put away or even left out for a child to come to when
she's ready to eat.

Nancy Samalin, author of *Loving Your Child is Not Enough,* told us the following story from Carol, a mother in one of her workshops: "Marvin, my twelve-year-old, came into the kitchen Saturday morning and said, 'Ma, I'm hungry.' I had decided that I was willing to cook that morning if anyone wanted anything hot so I said, 'Fine, what would you like to eat?' When he answered, 'Scrambled eggs,' I cooked them and gave him the plate. He looked at it and said, 'Yuk, I don't want these.' I told him, 'Marvin, I only cook once upon request. It's your choice to eat or not, but I'm not cooking anything else for you. If you don't want the eggs, help yourself to something you do want.' I turned back to what I was doing, and my son ate the eggs."

Carol did not allow herself to be manipulated. She also did not let her son's rejection of her proffered meal upset her or throw her off. She showed the child that she respected both his food choice and herself. She was not going to be a short-order cook. It was now up to Marvin to decide what he wanted to do.

It is also fine to decide how many items you want to prepare. No one wants to be a slave to the kitchen. It is wonderful for children to be very selective and specific, but that does not necessarily mean that every request must be met, especially if it leads to parents' oppression and eventual resentment. One five-year-old said to her mother, "I want bacon and eggs, then hot cereal and after that a baked apple." This mother responded, "I will cook one item for you. Choose which hot thing you would like to eat." She might set the limit at two cooked items. The number is unimportant. The important thing is that you stick to what you say. Then your child can assume the responsibility for choosing which dish gets cooked. If this child wanted eggs and cereal, you might have suggested that she have a raw apple if she was still hungry. This encourages her to eat what she knows her body is hungry for. She will also learn that there are adequate substitutes that validate the original need. Parenthetically, while it's not a rule, our observations indicate that children tend to be one- or two-item eaters. If you ask a child what she is really hungry for, it is usually one thing or at most two, the second food generally being associated with the first—peanut butter and jelly, meat and potatoes, bacon and eggs.

What Happens Away from Home?

It is important to take charge of the feeding situation and stick to this method when you are away from home. Family, friends and baby-sitters may want to deprive the child of certain food or stuff him, depending on their own eating habits or if they perceive the child as being either overweight or underweight. If, up until now, you have been limiting food intake or else pushing food, your relatives or your child's caretakers may continue to act the way you formerly did. Explain the changes you've made to people who are involved with the child and urge them to allow some leeway for this new feeding approach.

A full-time working mother at one of our workshops said, "I have a housekeeper who takes care of my eight-year-old son, Freddie. How can I get her to follow self-demand feeding when I'm not around?" We told this mother to explain the approach to the housekeeper and go over what changes would have to be made to implement it. These included allowing Freddie to have his own food shelf and allowing him free access to the refrigerator. We urged her to emphasize that it would be best if there were no comments made on Freddie's new eating behavior. We also suggested that she alert the housekeeper to some of the "unusual" eating conduct she might encounter—frequent/infrequent eating, unconventional food selections. The housekeeper should be prepared for a certain amount of testing as Freddie tries to determine if both parent and housekeeper are going to let him make these eating decisions.

Be ready for comments anyhow. It will be hard for people not familiar with self-demand feeding to accept, much less wholeheartedly support, your efforts. One grandmother, when confronted with her grandchild's new eating program, was reported to have said, "What do you mean she can eat when she is hungry and choose what she wants? In my house we eat at six, and I only cook once." In that case the parents had to decide how often the family would eat at Grandma's house and whether it was worth making an issue of the family's new food philosophy. They continued the regular Sunday visits but had to work with Grandma on the food issue. When the child was not hungry at dinner, they informed Grandma not to worry, since she would tell them when she was. They tried, at times, to make light of the situation but remembered to protect their child and their new endeavor. Before they left home, they asked their daughter what she thought she would like to eat later and brought those foods from home. In this way their child was able to eat what she wanted, and Grandma was not inconvenienced.

Another alternative is to explain to your child that Grandma does not understand your new way of eating and that it would be better not to make a big fuss while at her home. It may be best to avoid eating in the homes of relatives until your new style is well established or thoroughly explained and understood by the extended family.

It will also be necessary to teach your child how to ask for food at a friend's house. You will not always be around to run interference, and eventually the child will have to fend for himself in a way that feels comfortable.

Marilyn, the mother of Bill, age six, was dropping him off for a play date after school. While she was still in the kitchen with the other child's mother, Bill came in and told his friend's mother that he was hungry. The mother replied, "I'm making spaghetti for dinner, and it will be ready soon." Marilyn realized that "soon" was another twenty to thirty minutes and that Bill could not wait that long. She called Bill to her and said, "If you're hungry, why don't you ask Mrs. Graham if you could have a little something to tide you over until dinner." Bill asked for a piece of cheese and, of course, got it. It helps to teach your child to be specific in his food request and to indicate that he needs only "a little something" while waiting for dinner.

What About Setting Limits?

Up to now the rules you have imposed on your child regarding when, where, and how to eat probably reflect many of the limits that were imposed on you as a child. Setting limits may also be about what *you* can tolerate. For example, if you can't stand leftovers or anything going to waste, you may find yourself setting limits that keep a child from selecting quantity, with the fear that food will be wasted. Or you may force-feed your child so that nothing remains on his plate. It is important to avoid these automatic reactions to eating situations and to question whether the rule we set down is really necessary or whether it serves no real purpose beyond conforming to convention.

Take into account that different limits may be set at different times in a child's development as an eater. The fifteen-month-old should be allowed to play with her food because it is part of the environment she is exploring. She puts most things into her mouth and, given her level of coordination, drops half of what she touches. The five-year-old, however, should no longer be dropping food or using it as a toy.

There is a need, at times, to set firm limits that have nothing to do with food per se. We know that children must learn that they cannot have everything they may want or see. We do not live in a world of unlimited supply. Advertising is geared to produce "wanting" in children, and, as a result, they nag their parents to buy. If your child watches TV, you can expect her to be well versed in the latest cereals, toys, games, clothes and the like. You have both a right and a responsibility to help her understand that she cannot have everything she wants and that some items may not be good or age-appropriate for her.

As parents, we know how difficult supermarket shopping with a child can be. At most stores, near the checkout counter, sweets are at the child's eye and hand level, strategically placed so that children will ask or reach for them. It is hard to get into an extended discussion at that moment about whether your child is really hungry and what she is really hungry for. Probably the appearance of the sweet has triggered an interest not related to hunger. Even children steeped in the self-demand-feeding approach sometimes grab for sweets because they have learned from so many sources, particularly friends, that these candy bars are prized possessions. When self-demand feeding has been established, if given the candy, children will hold it or put it on their food shelves—but not eat it —or at least be in no rush to eat it.

We have found it extremely helpful to tell children *in advance* what the limits are. Margo was going to the store with her two children to buy groceries. She told each of them before they left the house that they could choose one item to buy at the store that was not already on the shopping list containing their food requests. After Alex had taken a cereal of his choice and Emily had chosen grape juice, their demands at the sweet counter were denied, even though the pressure was heavy. Margo stuck to her limit by reminding the children firmly of the understanding that they had reached before the shopping trip began. She did not allow them to buy candy on the street or pizza along the way—also part of the original "deal." It can be helpful to ask your children if they are hungry *before* you leave on a shopping trip, because then they can have the choice of eating before leaving the house or waiting until they get back.

At times, of course, the child will ask for food because he is actually hungry and it would be too long a wait until he got home. The issue to be addressed is whether the child wants the food he is asking for because he happens to see it or because of physical hunger. If the reason is hunger, several questions come up: Is it within your budget to buy the food he sees and wants? Is there enough variety at home from which he can choose? Will the wait be tolerable?

You'll need to respond differently in each situation, but not on the basis of a value judgment about the particular food the child is asking for. In other words, if you say that "chocolate bars are bad for you, so you'll have to wait until we get home for some granola bars," the message is quite different from, "There is chocolate waiting for you at home. We'll be there soon, so there's no need to buy any here."

Sometimes, when your child understands that her food requests will be honored, she may use the magic words "I am hungry" for other purposes. For example, one mother complained that her son, just at the moment of bedtime, invariably said he was hungry. Hunger demands shouldn't be allowed to manipulate the bedtime hour. We advised this mother to set up a routine so that, every evening, she informed her son when it was half an hour before bedtime. She told him that if he was hungry, *now* was the time to have a snack. He was also told that once bedtime came, he could no longer eat. Using this technique the family was able to enforce a "no eating at bedtime" rule and the actual bedtime hour without having to worry that the child would go to bed hungry. The same technique can be used with the child who wants a drink once he's in bed.

What Else Do I Need to Know?

Essential to the self-demand feeding approach is consistency. You are embarking on a long journey that can ultimately lead to peace and harmony around food and feeding. However, as you begin to introduce this approach, you must expect some turbulence. Children have difficulty, in general, with change.

Being consistent can be difficult for parents. Our daily lives are hectic. Demands, including those of our children, on our time and energy often seem relentless. Children are erratic, and sometimes our responses to them are equally erratic. Although we aim for consistency, our mood that particular morning, a disquieting phone call, a work problem unresolved, money worries or the car breaking down may cause us to respond unevenly to our children.

What happens when both parents don't agree on the use of self-demand feeding? You and your partner may have differing views on many aspects of self-demand feeding: legalizing foods, allowing sweets in the house, defining a balanced diet, insisting on family meals and generally giving up control over what, when and how much your children eat. Take plenty of time to discuss how this approach will work in your family. Talk about the pros and cons with regard to life-style and current pressures. Evaluate how different this program is from the current eating pattern in your household and see if (a) you are willing to take on the commitment; and (b) what changes will need to be made and in what order. Reread portions of this book together. Perhaps you can get a few parents to form a group and work out your differences in the group.

Needless to say, parental unity is important to the success of this approach. Your child needs a clear message from you if this is going to work in your home. We wouldn't recommend starting until you and your mate clear up any differences you may have about implementing self-demand feeding.

You will have to take a very close look at your own eating practices. If you are obsessed with food, eating and body size or if you are an on-again, off-again dieter, bringing all kinds of foods into your house may feel scary. You may think that you yourself will be out of control. Do you feel you can give your child freedom around food and eating while denying it to yourself? (We believe that the very best circumstance for applying this approach to a child is when the parents are following it as well.)

How do you feel about letting your child determine when and what s/he wants to eat? If you need to be in control of your child's eating, then this approach is not for you. We saw in chapter two how the myths that surround the feeding situation create more problems than they solve. Even so, giving up your attachments to these old ways takes time and effort. And you can be sure that a number of situations will arise that will test your ability to be consistent in applying the self-demand feeding approach with your child.

Your child will almost certainly, at first, go after the "special" goodies that have been denied. It may take great control and resolve on your part to allow your child to eat her way through these foods. Take courage! Her fixation on these newly legalized foods will diminish and finally disappear. Your consistency in making these foods available at her request will shorten the time it takes. (See chapter six, "The Undaunted Sweet Tooth.")

In the initial stages of this approach some children, though not all, will put on weight. They may experience the new freedom to eat but not yet have the ability to identify hunger or fullness. Some overeating and the possible attendant weight gain are unsettling to many parents, especially if their child is overweight to start with or if the parents themselves are preoccupied with their own weight. However, when children understand that this approach is here to stay—that they will always be able to have what they are hungry for—the overeating subsides. The feeling of license gives way to a feeling of security, and they begin to eat in concert with their needs. Once again, your consistency is essential in making this possible. We have seen overweight children gain no weight at all with self-demand feeding. Others have stabilized after the initial testing period is over.

Consistency also requires giving the child wide latitude to discover her own likes and dislikes in food. Your child's ability to make and trust her own choices depends on your not questioning or ridiculing what she wants, no matter how odd it seems.

As children learn about the world through experimentation, they also need to learn about food through experimentation. This may involve eating combinations of foods that are unpalatable to others. Betsy, age four, decided that she liked milk and apple juice mixed together. Her mother, Harriet's, first reaction was, "Oh, how disgusting! What happens if she does that at other people's homes?" Harriet was quite familiar with the self-demand feeding approach and decided to refrain from saying out loud what she was thinking. Instead she came up with a creative solution that showed respect for Betsy's explorations. Harriet said to Betsy, "I see you've come up with a new drink. It's fine to mix apple juice and milk at home, but when you go to your grandma's, she may question you because most people don't drink the two together. It's fine to do it here, though."

Children will go through "food phases." If hot dogs have become a favorite item, allow the phase to run its course, and be sure to have hot dogs in good supply. If food choices seem "odd"—mustard sandwiches were one boy's specialty—again, allow the "odd" choice, and be sure to have the necessary ingredients on hand.

The consistent support of self-demand feeding, once underway, will yield great rewards and, in the long run, will take less time and energy than any other feeding approach we know. To live without battles raging over endless parental orders ("Eat this," "Don't eat that," "First your potatoes," "Clean your plate," "Dessert comes after dinner") and without children's relentless counterdemands will be a welcome relief. The real payoff is to see your child developing a relaxed and comfortable relationship to food, free of the constraints and anxieties that plague so many people.

6

THE UNDAUNTED
SWEET TOOTH

It is a clear, crisp, star-studded evening. Throughout the land you can see the slow movements of witches, goblins, superheroes, princesses and ghosts. Preparation for this day of fantasy began weeks ago. Costumes had to be made, lines memorized for school plays, pumpkins carved and decorated and treats bought in great quantity. Finally children, transformed into haunting or comical creatures, hit the streets shouting, *"Trick or treat!"* They are filled with enthusiasm, life and joy. With shameless abandon they demand goodies to fill their hands, mouths, pockets, bags and knapsacks. Their parents are either in quick pursuit or anxiously awaiting their return home.

More sweets are consumed on Halloween than on any other day of the year. This candy mania is publicly sanctioned, even encouraged, and most children love Halloween because it is the day they are licensed to eat sweets. They feel they have to get all that candy in now before the supply ends or the license expires. When we held a workshop for parents the week following Halloween, the stories were distressingly similar: Beth, the mother of seven-year-old Tasha, told us she was absolutely convinced that all the Halloween sugar had made her daughter "jumpy and irritable." Another parent described the aftermath of Halloween as a "living hell." For days, her child's mind did not wander for a moment from his candy stash. Yet another upset mother reported that the battles that ensued about which sweets could be consumed far surpassed in intensity all prior struggles about food.

Only one was different. A parent who had never put any restrictions on sweets told the group that her eight-year-old daughter had very little interest in her Halloween candy. She said, "Jackie was much more preoccupied with planning and making her costume. She kept talking about surprising the neighbors in her costume and wondering if they would recognize her. When she returned home Halloween night, she went through her bag of candy, separated the kinds she liked from those she didn't like and planned to give away the kinds she didn't like. And you know what? Most of the candy is still in the house."

Jackie's reaction may seem unique, but it is the result of growing up with self-demand feeding. In her house it was Halloween all year round. Sweets had never been forbidden. To her candy was nice, but having it was not an unusual event.

Because sugar has been such a problem in many families, it may be hard to believe that it *is* possible for children to be relaxed around sweets *if* they are treated like any other food. In order to understand the importance of "legalizing" sweets, we need to backtrack and unravel the Halloween problem.

Tasha had become jumpy and irritable as a result of eating so many sweets. In Tasha's house sweets were rarely allowed, and following Halloween night, her parents gave her forty-eight hours to eat the candy she had collected. After this time, the remaining candy would be thrown away. With this restriction held over Tasha's head, she frantically ate nothing but candy for two days. Who wouldn't? And guess what? She became visibly more tense and irritable. She was not fun to be around. Before Halloween, Tasha was a calm, charming, rather quiet little girl. Now she had become an out-of-control little "monster." Why did Tasha's personality change?

To begin with, the body reacts to any food consumed in great quantity. The quantity eaten in those forty-eight hours after Halloween had shocked her system. Had she been eating carbohydrates, proteins or fats in such great quantity for two days, there would have been side effects as well. It wasn't the sugar per se that was the culprit, it was the overuse of it.

The threat that all these sweets would be taken away quite predictably made Tasha frantic and irritable. She didn't understand why she had to throw these treats away. It made her angry that she'd have to wait a whole year to get another supply that would, once again, be allowed in her grasp only momentarily. She felt under great pressure to consume as much as she possibly could and was eating way beyond any feelings of hunger. Her parents' rule seemed quite irrational to her and caused much confusion and distress.

Brian's mother told him that he could keep all his Halloween loot and choose two sweets each day until it ran out. She reported, "I can't tell you what living hell it was. Every morning started with 'I want candy.' Sometimes I'd say, 'Okay, but remember, you'll only have one more to go for today.' He asked for candy from the minute he got home from school until bedtime. He seemed like a candy junkie waiting for his next fix. The battles were unending and made us crazy."

Brian's singleminded interest in his Halloween candies was caused as much by their forbidden quality and limited supply as by their taste. The procedures of doling his candy out in restricted amounts both heightened and frustrated his desire. When something is forbidden, it attracts intense interest. In times of food rationing or shortage, the food that is not available becomes a much-desired luxury, like bananas in England during World War II or liquor during Prohibition.

Brian's mother, like many parents, felt that she could not trust him with sweets. She said, "If I left it to his own choice, he would eat only sweets." Many parents convey strong messages of distrust to their children: "If you're not kept in check, you will turn into little pigs shoveling sweets in your mouths nonstop."

Often these parents have a point. When sweets have been restricted, children will go after them fast and furiously when they first become available. This response is not due to the child's "innate wildness," but is rather a normal and predictable response to the prior deprivation. The natural response to food deprivation is to binge on precisely the food that has been off limits. As those of you who have ever tried to lose weight know, at the end of a diet you never binge on the foods that were permitted; you turn to the forbidden foods.

When sweets are forbidden or hidden in the house, sneak eating becomes first a game and eventually a habit. Children experience pleasure and power in "putting one over" on the parents when they find where the secret stash of candy is hidden or get some away from home. But the pleasure and power are often accompanied by the fear of being bad, getting caught or the worry of how to replace what was taken. Adults with compulsive-eating problems are quite familiar with this pattern as well as the accompanying feelings.

One parent told us, "Look, I feel that sweets, in general, are unhealthy, but I figured that some treats in their bag were less harmful than others. So, this Halloween I tempered my ideas by allowing Felicia and Bryn to divide their loot up into candy that was good and candy that was bad. There was a lot of tension in the house because the kids often wanted what I considered bad candy. I've certainly said no to them before, but they were never quite so upset."

We explained to this parent that the children were reacting to the labels. We call sweet foods bad or junk to discourage the child and ourselves from eating them. Then, if the child eats these foods anyhow, she may feel as if *she* is bad. Children are in the process of forming their identity and are often preoccupied with issues of good and bad. They want to please mommy and daddy. If they eat something you disapprove of and negatively label, they feel your displeasure and think the label applies to them. This adds to the confusion about sweets that most children experience: They feel deprived if they don't eat sweets and damned if they do.

Often parents try to scare children away from sweets or other foods with strong warnings about their dangerous effects. Literal interpretations of this "danger" may cause much more distress than was intended. Louise, the mother of two children ages three and eight, shared this story with us: "I believe that we should eliminate sugar from our diet in addition to eliminating many chemical additives. I have told my children from a very early age that many of these things are bad and poisonous and may lead to cancer. My eight-year-old, without me knowing it, would go with his friends after school and use his allowance to buy candy. When a friend's father died of cancer, my son was upset for weeks. Since we barely knew the man, we couldn't understand why he was so affected until, several weeks later, he came to us to confess his candy-eating ritual. He was sure he was going to die soon because of the 'poison' he was eating."

It goes without saying that we have a responsibility to teach our children what is good in our environment and what is harmful. However, we must be sensitive to what a child can handle. Information should be given in a way that is not overwhelming or terrifying. As we know, children's minds are quite literal: To label as a poison something that may have ill effects when eaten in excess can unnecessarily scare a child. Sugar, for example, is not a poison.

Children should not be offered anything that *is* harmful. Just as we wouldn't want a toddler playing with matches, we don't want our children drinking polluted water or eating foods with carcinogens in them. Be sure, however, that what you prohibit as "harmful" is truly that. Many foods that are not harmful have been given that label merely because they are less nutritious than some other foods—junk foods, for example. This labeling interferes with a child's ability to make food selections.

How can we educate our children about good nutrition without inducing guilt or undue fear? If your child insists on eating Cap'n Crunch cereal on a daily basis, what can you do? Surely, you can give your opinion that Cap'n Crunch is not the most nutritious cereal and explain why you believe this. You can offer other cereal choices. If you present your point of view in a way that is not coercive but in the spirit of gentle guidance, there will be a greater chance your child will hear you. Even so, your child may continue to insist on Cap'n Crunch. If he's made to feel guilty for it, communication will break down. We have to trust that children learn through their own experiences and arrive at their own conclusions. In many areas we have to let our children experiment. This can be anxiety-producing for us as parents, but it can also eliminate power struggles and help children grow up with greater self-confidence and security. If you have made choices about certain foods, you have to trust that your child will most likely make similar choices if he is not deprived or forced to make them.

What do you think would happen if you allowed your children to go to the supermarket and buy whatever they wanted?

After attending our post-Halloween workshop, one father decided to try the self-demand feeding method even though the freedom around sweets made him nervous. He had the following conversation with his four-year-old twin daughters:

BOB: We are going to the supermarket, and you can buy whatever you want.

NELL: Can we have candy?

BOB: Yes.

KATE: Pretzels and potato chips?

BOB: Of course, and we should buy a big supply.

NELL: What happens when it's all gone?

BOB: Tell me before it's all gone and we'll get more. Also, each of you will have your own food shelf where you will put those favorite foods. You don't have to share them with each other or with us.

KATE: Will you tell Mommy not to eat our food?

BOB: Yes!

KATE: I want to find that round candy my teacher gave me in school.

They enter the market.

NELL: I want potato chips. How many bags should I get?

BOB: *(since they are small)* Get four.

NELL: *(eyes wide with disbelief)* I also want candy. I'll buy Tootsie Rolls. Should I get two bags?

BOB: Yes, that's fine.

NELL: Oh, I think one will be enough.

BOB: Better get two to be sure.

KATE: I want Cheese Doodles, two big bags, and Fritos, two small bags. Daddy, this looks like the candy my teacher had. What's in them?

BOB: This one is peppermint; this one is fruit filled; and these are sour balls.

KATE: They're not right. I'll just have some gold fish.

NELL: I want ginger snap cookies too.

BOB: Do you want any ice cream?

KATE
and
NELL: Yes. Chocolate, vanilla and coffee.

BOB: Do you want anything else?

NELL: Fruit. Cherries and bananas.
KATE: Watermelon and apricots.

Both children asked the vegetable man for two handfuls of small apricots. They went to the checkout counter, and each child was given her own bag of goodies to carry home. They ate apricots on the way home. When they got home, they cleared two low shelves in the cupboard and spent quite a while marking their turf and arranging their sweets. Nell ate one cookie and Kate asked for a Tootsie Roll from Nell's supply. They bargained back and forth and decided that since they had bought great quantities of different items, they could do some trading and still have enough of their original stock. In the next few hours they opened and shut the shelf door a hundred times, but mostly they just looked at the supply. The next morning each selected some of the cookies they bought, ate a few and then asked for ice cream. When Bob opened the freezer, the girls saw the three flavors they had bought the day before as well as homemade yogurt pops. They chose the yogurt pops.

Two weeks later there still was no need to shop for more sweets. Who would have believed it? These children did not want everything in sight and did not always choose the sweets on their food shelves when they wanted something to eat.

Bob's experience is quite common. When favorite foods are available, children can feel secure. However, if food restrictions have been vigorously enforced and a switch is being made to self-demand feeding, sometimes a child will binge with this new-found freedom. Try not to worry: With consistent use of self-demand feeding the binging will taper off.

Is Sugar Fattening?

If we had to select one food most surrounded with prejudices, myths and terror, surely it would be sugar. What are the causes of this terror? We are afraid of getting fat; we think sugar is harmful; we think it causes tooth decay and hyperactivity; we are certain that sugar is addictive.

Let's begin by looking at the connection between sweets and weight gain. We are a nation obsessed with slimness. New diets and strategies for weight loss hit us at a rapid-fire rate.

Whatever we are told is fattening we think is bad and we should deprive ourselves of these bad foods. But what does *fattening* mean? Although it is true that different foods have different caloric values, no particular food or food groups make us fat. *It is not sugar that makes us fat.* What makes us fat is *overeating. If we eat more than our physiological hunger calls for, we gain weight.* Many people have had the experience of being on a diet that allowed unlimited quantities of certain foods. They found that at the end of a week of being "good" on the diet, they did not lose weight, but may even have gained some as a result of overeating the unlimited foods.

Is Sugar Harmful?

No food eaten in excess is good for us. Too much of any one food tends to cause us to diminish our intake of other foods and can sometimes lead to serious dietary deficiency or excess and to actual medical problems. Remember the people who became sick or died on the protein diet? Our bodies need a full range of foods, and to deprive them of one food group or to flood them with another will not maintain ideal health. It is a mistake to think that we will get thin or maintain good health merely by eliminating sugar from our diet.

Sugar is not the most caloric food around. Far from it. A tablespoon of white granulated sugar has 45 calories while a tablespoon of butter has 100 calories. It should be noted that some of the harmful additives in our world are the sugar *substitutes*. Jane Brody in *The New York Times*, April 4, 1984, states that "a switch from refined table sugar (sucrose) to honey cannot be justified on health or nutritional grounds. Tablespoon for tablespoon, honey has eighteen more calories than sugar: its nutrient content is too minuscule to matter; it rots teeth faster than sugar and it sometimes contains carcinogens." Brody also points out that "among artificial sweeteners, saccharin promotes cancer growth in laboratory animals and the long-term safety of aspertane (Equal or Nutrisweet) has not been established. Both perpetuate a desire for very sweet foods."

People are concerned about sweets being harmful because all they have seen and experienced is their own and others' irrepressible desire for this substance, which has always been off limits. Again, it is not sweets per se that are harmful. *It is the abuse of sweets, the predictable outcome of their "forbidden" quality, that causes damage.* It may sound fantastic, but if every day were Halloween, there would be little fear of sugar and little sugar abuse.

Does Sugar Cause Tooth Decay?

One of the most common concerns about giving sweets to children is the fear of tooth decay. Some studies show that sugar seems to cause more caries if left on teeth than foods with less sugar. If your child's diet only contained sweets, his teeth might rot. But the health and strength of teeth are dependent primarily on heredity and a complex interaction between food consistency, eating frequency, brushing and flossing habits and fluoride intake. Dentists say again and again that tooth decay is fostered primarily by food remaining on the teeth for a period of time.

Do Sweets Lead to Hyperactivity in Children?

Many parents and physicians feel that too much sugar consumption in children leads to altered behavior. As we saw in our first Halloween example, the child's hyperactivity seemed to be a result of being let out of a cage vis-à-vis sweets. She was experiencing a brief moment of escape and was frantically trying to stave off a return to "jail." Eating a larger quantity of sweets than the body can handle is often a cause of hyperactivity, as is the frantic atmosphere around foods that are forbidden.

We have discovered, however, that the hyperactivity that parents attribute to sweets often stems from other sources. True, on the surface the child seems to be eating a lot of sweets and is simultaneously hyperactive. This combination of factors —the eating of sweets and the hyperactivity—is not necessarily cause and effect. Sometimes the excessive amount of sweets and the hyperactivity both stem from another source. Let us tell you an illustrative story: Stacy, the mother of eight-year-old Brad, was told by her physician to take Brad off all sugar products because he had become very jumpy, difficult to handle, combative, negative and in general hard to live with. When we met Stacy at a workshop, she described the difficulty she was having attempting to follow this no-sugar diet. We asked her to think back to when her son's behavior had changed. Had there been any significant changes in his life at that time? She said, "This was six months before my husband and I separated. It was a time when we began to argue very frequently and openly. There was an awful lot of tension in our house."

How often do we notice our children's sudden changed behavior and assume that the change in their eating habits is the culprit rather than a clue that something is troubling them? Many people are currently looking at the relationship between sugar and hyperactivity. Some people are suggesting that some of us may even be allergic or particularly sensitive to sugar and sugar products. No doubt there are all kinds of reactions to food substances that we will learn more about in the future.

Certainly, if your child were to develop any unusual behavior, you would want to have it checked out medically. If you are concerned about your child's diet, investigate all possible sources of information. The point is that it is very hard for anyone to know the real story about hyperactivity if sweets are a special or forbidden food. What we do know for sure is that anyone, child or adult, will respond to deprivation with increased desire for whatever has been put off limits. Until your child is living free in a world of food, certain that sweets will always be available, there is no way to know if his hyperactivity is a reaction to sugar or simply the predictable response to being "let out of jail" and to consuming larger quantities than the body can normally handle.

Are Sweets Addictive?

Underlying all parental fears is the assumption that children, if allowed free access to sweets, would misuse this freedom and become insatiable. As we know, most adults are terrified of sweets. People who diet say, "I never keep sweets in the house, and if I do, I hide them." Or, "I went to a party last week, and wouldn't you know, a plate of chocolates was next to me. I couldn't stop eating them. I pigged out and felt so guilty."

"When my eight-year-old asks me to buy him a chocolate bar, I say no because I feel scared to have chocolate anywhere near me." "Since I am perpetually on a diet, I do not want sweets around."

Sweets are everywhere, and most of us spend a great deal of time and energy trying to avoid them. It's clear that their mystique carries over from childhood. Imagine a full-grown person feeling that candy emits a magnetic force. Sweets are given a power and meaning seldom placed on any other food, and this is what leads to both their attraction and their abuse. When they are no longer used as a treat, bribe ("Sit still in the doctor's office and you'll get an ice cream later"), or threat ("You can't have dessert if you don't listen to me"), we will have a world where ice cream is equal to salad.

Letting go of all the rules about sweets is easier said than done. If, as parents, *we* hide from cookies, then we are going to worry about our children's welfare in a land of sweets. Yet we know from years of experience with both children and adults that your worst fears about what would happen if sweets were readily available are unfounded. When any food is truly available, physically and psychologically, it loses its magic. The going may be a little rough at first—children have trouble believing that sweets will never be taken away from them again—but after a sufficient number of bags of M&Ms, the interest subsides.

When there is an abundant supply of all foods, children don't turn to any one food and misuse it. Placing foods into certain camps—good for you, bad for you; dinner foods, snack foods— paves the way for eating struggles. Children prefer snacking over eating meals. If dinner foods could join the snack-food camp, there would not be such an overuse of sweets. Children reach for sweets without thinking; they are readily available, attractively presented and quite manageable. If other snack choices were as ready to hand—fruit salads, yogurt pops, bags of nuts, cereal, raisins, tuna salad, deviled eggs, cold chicken, raw vegetables—they would be chosen more often.

Many parents worry about what looks to them like a craving for sweets—once you eat them, you seem to crave more. We have found in our work that this craving is often psychological in origin. If you have gone for long periods without sweets, you then "go crazy" once they're in sight. Our clients, both children and adults, have proven that once sweets join the category of *just another food*, the craving and the need subside.

At some point you must take the plunge. Try experimenting with yourself first. You might want to see what would happen if you had your most-craved or forbidden food available to you, both in your head and on your own shelf. See how long it will take for the magic to disappear. Once you've tried the approach, you may be less hesitant to begin it with your children. It may be that your children will go wild for a few weeks or even a few months. But if you stick to your story—no double messages—and follow our approach, you will see that they will stop abusing sugar.

REMEMBER:
- Give each child her own shelf.
- Allow each child to choose whatever sweets and other foods he wants.
- Point out dwindling supplies long before they run out. This demonstrates to your child that you mean what you say about never-ending supplies.
- Relax. Do not interfere.

7

ATTUNEMENT: KNOWING WHAT CHILDREN NEED

Charlie's parents have lectured endlessly on the importance of eating green, leafy vegetables, yet Charlie refuses to eat anything that is even faintly green. Although Maggie has been told that milk is an essential part of a growing child's diet, she rejects milk. It seems to make her sick and cranky. Brian, age two, is perfectly able to drink from a cup but still demands his bottle. Kira, an eight-year-old, knows how to get her own breakfast but insists that her mother prepare it for her. Michael, at ten, no longer wants to join the family for dinner, but would rather eat his meal in front of the television. Karen's mother decides to surprise her fifteen-year-old with her favorite supper food, and she refuses to eat. Situations like these can be maddening for parents. We may grit our teeth, pull our hair, and silently scream, "What do these children want, anyway?"

To answer this question parents must try to put aside their preconceptions and tune into their child. This process is called attunement. It is not magical; most parents are more or less attuned to their child already. Unfortunately, in the area of food, our culture teaches us not to listen to the signals. We are instructed to feed our child three meals a day with foods from the four basic food groups, to serve desserts at the end of a meal, to avoid sweets whenever possible. We are so indoctrinated with these cultural biases and myths that we sometimes lose track of the child's individuality. Rather than fitting our children into society's rigid rules about food and eating, let's try to understand their real needs.

Learning your child's cues and signals can start at birth. Many hospitals now have "rooming-in," where mother, infant and sometimes father stay in the same room as soon as the baby is born. Greater recognition of the importance of early parent-infant bonding has prompted this change. The mother fills her infant's needs for food, warmth and contact, and the infant begins to acquaint herself with the smell, touch and taste of this nurturing person.

One mother described her hospital experience in which there was no rooming-in: "When I was in the hospital, I was told the baby would be brought to me every four hours to be fed. I heard screams coming from the nursery an hour before feeding time. When I asked the nurse why so many of the babies, including mine, were crying, she said not to worry. 'Babies cry a lot; they are just exercising their lungs.' I asked if perhaps the babies were hungry. A look was thrown my way, and I felt dismissed as another overanxious, new mother. I wondered if the hospital staff knew what was best for me and my baby."

What is a newborn's cry about? What does the infant need? Was this mother "overanxious" or was she accurate in her interpretation of her baby's cries? How are hunger cries different from wet cries? When does an infant need feeding rather than holding and rocking? Slowly, these questions get answered. We begin to figure out what our baby's cry means.

The first step of attunement is recognizing the uniqueness of this one special baby. Just as parents bring their own strengths, limitations, and hopes to the job of parenting, so each baby brings his capacities for responsiveness, activity and growth. In any hospital nursery you will see great variations in temperament, alertness, sound of cry . . . . Listen to parents talk and you will hear about the uniqueness of their infants. "My baby is so good, she sleeps for hours between feedings," or "My baby is quite restless, he prefers short naps and eats small amounts very frequently." From the first few moments following birth, children show us their special nature, a specialness that continues all their lives. As parents we must understand that our children will develop in their own way and at their own unique pace.

Your ability to respond to the particular needs of your child will naturally be affected by your *own* needs, strengths and limits. As one new mother explained, "In the first few weeks with Jesse I noticed that he wanted to nurse at the breast much, much longer on some days than on others. Rather than forcing a schedule on him, I let him decide how often he would be nursed. Fortunately, his needs comfortably met mine. I wanted to be with Jesse, to get to know him, to look at him, to marvel at him and to feel myself respond to him."

Such an easy meshing doesn't always happen, as another mother's story illustrates: "Since I was ten and saw my cousin breast-feed her first child, I had wanted to breast-feed. When I gave birth to my daughter, I began to breast-feed, and as it turned out, my baby thrived, but I was miserable. During the first six weeks I had a couple of bouts of mastitis and eventually a breast abscess. I thought about stopping, but I was in terrible conflict because of my own ideal and because it was 1979, when breast-feeding was very much in vogue. Then my midwife pointed out that these notions of mine were getting in the way of reality. Since I was suffering, my baby was not getting the closeness and the good feeding experience she needed. All of my physical problems were actually keeping me from getting close to my baby. The midwife was right, but still I was sad when I bound my breasts and turned to bottles."

Attunement between you and your child lays the groundwork for your child to grow up with a clear and defined understanding of who she is. If your baby cries because she needs holding and physical contact and you respond by showing her a toy or giving her food, she will continue to cry because her need has not been met. If you hold and cuddle your baby and this accurate response happens with some consistency, she will learn two valuable lessons. First, she learns that she has a need for warmth and contact. Second, she learns that her needs can be understood and met. Her sense of herself as a separate person will grow.

How often have you seen a cracker stuffed in the mouth of a crying child without anyone trying to find out what the crying is really about? A child who is frightened when he goes for his first haircut is often offered a lollipop. One pediatrician we know has a gumdrop tree, and after a child gets a shot, candies are pulled off the tree and offered. When a child's distress is inappropriately met with food, the child learns that food is a substitute for soothing words and reassuring hugs. These are not attuned responses because they are unrelated to the child's actual needs.

Attunement also requires an understanding of how your child grows and develops. You will need patience, flexibility and sensitivity as your child follows his own course and his own timetable in becoming an independent person. Growth takes place with forward and backward steps; there are pauses, struggles, accomplishments, and frustrations.

A baby moves from a state of oneness with mother to becoming a separate person in the world. One day your baby is clingy, the next day she is a little explorer. One day your child can button her sweater, and the next day she needs mommy to do it. One day she insists you take her to the school door, and the next day she goes off on the bus without even turning back for a final wave. The experience with food and feeding follows a similar developmental course.

Except in rare cases, everyone's first experience with food is connected to the feeder—usually mother. Feeding starts as part of a relationship between two people—it is about love and connection, not only meeting hunger. The infant's experience of oneness with the parent is essential for his or her development. It is also blissful for the child as well as for many parents. As the infant grows, the shift to more separation brings about changes for you, your child and the feeding situation. The baby must start to face the world. The parent, too, must let go of this very tight connection.

Your child will learn to go from bottle to cup, from playing with food to eating with proper table manners, from eating baby food to eating grownup food and from being fed to feeding herself. These developments involve a gain and a loss. Though she loses the close connection she once had with you, she gains a strong sense of achievement at being able to master and control her environment. Watch your child's face as she masters the spoon, feeds herself and takes her spoon to feed you. She is proud and happy. At this stage food is becoming an object separate from the feeder.

58

As your child enters the second year of life, she has less physical hunger but a new hunger for the world. Great elation accompanies this heightened appetite. Your child is beginning to walk; she is able to hold objects with greater confidence and has a keen interest in her environment. You hear more and more the phrase "me do it."

Attunement is working well when parents can watch for their child's physical and psychological readiness, offer a push forward where appropriate, watch for the child's response to that gentle push, and then take cues from the child once again. In feeding a thirteen-month-old, the process might look like this: You offer the child a cup, and repeatedly he throws it on the floor or knocks it over. He has no interest in drinking from it. You offer it again in a few days, but without any pressure to use it. This is the gentle push. One day you notice that he grabs for your coffee cup. He is apparently ready for a cup. You get the child's training cup, fill it with juice and offer it. He is interested for a short period of time and then returns to the bottle. This is fine. There is no reason to force the baby to stay with the cup. He may forget the cup for a few days, and then the process will be repeated. The baby's involvement with the bottle and the cup has to do with his need to suck, his agility, hand-eye coordination and other factors. Understanding this and allowing development to take its course is what attunement is about.

Staying in tune can sometimes be trying. We have often heard a parent say, "I hate giving our one-year-old her spoon because she makes such a terrible mess." While this is true, you may be saying more to the child than "I do not enjoy cleaning up messes." Your one-year-old, seated in her high chair and being fed applesauce, grabs for the jar and puts her fingers in it. You quickly remove the jar from her reach, say no and clean up the mess. She wonders what happened. Next she sees the yogurt you are about to offer. Some spills on her high chair, and she smears it on her tray. Again, you clean it up with a no. Now she is angry and wonders why she is constantly being interrupted in her explorations. Deciding to have nothing more to do with your interference, she refuses to eat. You are upset that she is not eating and not quite sure why. She refuses the food because she wants to feed herself, not because she isn't hungry.

Your one-year-old is not ready for neatness and table manners. She needs to play with food and explore its qualities. She sees food as an object to be enjoyed, handled, thrown, sucked, spit out and most assuredly messed with. In order for her to gain mastery and control over her feeding, she must be allowed this exploration without constant interruptions.

During the next few years your child will experience remarkable changes—gaining significant mobility and independence. She will go from crawling to walking, from individual play to group play, from attachment to mother to interaction with peers. Her relationship to food will also change drastically —from being fed to feeding herself. While there will be many more foods on her menu, she can be quite selective. She may choose a narrow range of foods, select or reject particular foods, eat at a pace different than others. Attunement in the eating arena means giving her the necessary leeway to be self-defined and in charge.

A mother of a four-year-old said, "Noah has gotten to a point where he won't eat any foods with the slightest bit of seasoning because he says, 'There is dirt on this food.' " Noah's mother did not make an issue of his dislike of spices. She did not try to convince him that spices weren't dirt. She respected his growing need to make his own decisions and choices; she felt that his distaste of seasonings was an expression of his developing independence and didn't have much to do with food.

Abe, age seven, will only eat the foods that his daddy likes. Why? Attunement to this child's identification with his dad is very important. He is going through a stage where he wants to imitate his father in all areas. He wants to carry a satchel to school the way his father carries a briefcase to work. He likes to change when he gets home from school; his father changes out of his business clothes when he comes home from the office. The attuned parent allows the child to play out this phase of his development. With respect to food, Abe's mother might say, "I know you like doing what Daddy does, and that's perfectly okay, but each of us has different tastes, and yours may be different from Daddy's even though you love and admire him. You can copy a lot of the things Daddy does, but if you feel like eating something different, that would be just fine."

When your child is eight or nine, he may be preoccupied with what his peers are doing. You are concerned about his social and emotional as well as his physical needs. Therefore, when he tells you that he won't eat bologna sandwiches anymore because his best friend doesn't like meat, you understand this shift in his food choices. Again, attunement means understanding what his meat refusal *really* means—imitation of peers. Allow him to go through this phase; let him know there may be other options, but respect his choice.

As your child grows older, he may make strange food selections, reject certain foods, eat at unusual times and in unusual places. This is a natural part of his gaining independence from you and part of forming his own identity. One mother, a gourmet cook, told workshop participants that her ten-year-old son insisted on eating ravioli sandwiches for lunch everyday. She would have preferred quiche and salad or a roast beef sandwich for him, but she allowed him to make his own choices. Months later he had switched to a steady diet of tuna fish sandwiches but eventually developed a much more varied appetite. By letting her son make his own food choices, this mother encouraged his independence and decision-making ability. She avoided having food selection become a struggle for control.

Children often use the feeding situation to work through numerous issues that have nothing to do with food or hunger. Remember Charlie and Maggie in the opening paragraph who would not eat the "essential" foods offered by their parents? This struggle had little if anything to do with vegetables and milk. They were using food just as they might use bedtime, toileting, clothes, friendship or toys to exercise control, an important aspect of establishing identity. Brian and Kira would not feed themselves because they wanted mommy or daddy to do it for them. They were using the feeding situation in order to maintain a close connection to their parents. Michael and Karen, by refusing to eat at the table and rejecting the "favorite" foods, were either testing out separation from their parents or perhaps seeking attention and, therefore, connection in a provocative way. In each of these cases food became enmeshed with normal issues of dependence, independence, authority, control and identity. The challenge parents face is to be attuned to the child's real concerns and to avoid letting the eating behavior become the focus.

Three-year-old Sally wanted her mother to spoon-feed her

even though she was quite able to feed herself. Sally's mother had just given birth to her second child, and Sally was using the feeding situation to try to reclaim her mother's waning attention. When Sally's mother caught on to her child's concern, she stopped pressing Sally to use her spoon and allowed her to regress in her eating habits while assuring her that she would always be the special first child.

Sometimes the underlying issues are a mystery that we are unable to resolve. Seven-year-old Jonathan only ate four foods: cereal, ice cream, peanut butter and pizza. His parents tried everything they could think of to get him to eat other things. They played games, cajoled, mixed new foods with his favorites, but nothing worked. Despite his limited menu, Jonathan was a healthy child, but his mother and father felt that they would be "bad" parents if they didn't broaden his food intake. We asked if they could remember going through similar phases as children, and, sure enough, Jonathan's father remembered that he had insisted on wearing his baseball hat in the house, at school and even when he went to bed. Jonathan was doing the same thing with food that his father had done with the baseball hat: He was searching for a sense of personal control. Respect for his food choices will help him along that path. The key is not to make food a cause célèbre in the household.

Parents of teenagers know how difficult it is to be attuned. It can feel like a living hell to share space with an adolescent. Their minds change constantly; they are in a peer culture that at times is mystifying or frightening; they want independence and yet they can be very childish and irresponsible. Developmentally teenagers are working through their ultimate separation from you. They want freedom, but at the same time, the sought-after independence is scary. Their bodies are changing. Their sexuality is unfolding, and they are excited and worried. They can eat you out of house and home or they can starve themselves. Being sensitive to the way your teenager expresses and deals with these issues can help the youngster's development. (More on this in chapter twelve.)

Attunement to every stage of your child's life is critical for her personal growth, including the development of a healthy relationship to food. With this kind of awareness you will avoid family food struggles when the underlying issues have nothing to do with food. Your child will be permitted to make her own choices and develop her own tastes, at her own rate. Finally, your attuned responses will allow her to develop inner controls. This will occur when you validate her decisions and she feels confirmed as a separate person. Essential to self-demand feeding is the child's growing ability to recognize and take responsibility for her own decisions. She can develop this control with your compassionate guidance.

8

OVERCOMING OBSTACLES: PERCEPTIONS OF FOOD AND APPEARANCE

Incorporating self-demand feeding into your life will naturally present some problems. When you change your views on traditions and social rules, the transition may not go smoothly. Food is more than just a source of nourishment. It was the connecting substance in the earliest relationship with parents and it is an important expression of cultural, ethnic, and religious traditions.

In order to help your children grow up free in a world of food, you will need to separate your own food and body biases from those of your children. Step one in this process is to recall your own eating history. It may be helpful to ask yourself these following questions:

- What are your earliest memories of how food was handled in your house?
- What rules did your parents have about eating?
- Were there problems or conflicts about your eating? Were other family members involved? How were these issues dealt with?
- What are your current concerns about your eating and/ or your body size?

By looking at your own history, you can begin to understand why your relationship to food is so complicated. This understanding can help you approach the feeding of your children differently.

Family Background

Each of us grew up in a family whose particular situation or history affected our relationship to food. Some of our parents lived through the food scarcities of the depression or World War II or other difficult situations. In many instances these experiences led them to regard the robust, chubby child as a symbol of health and plenty. Advertisements like the Gerber baby or the Campbell soup twins proudly displayed chubby infants. Food was pushed on children in the belief that the more they ate, the healthier and happier they would be. Many of us who were raised this way never learned what it feels like to be hungry, and as adults we have great difficulty knowing when to eat and when to stop. We say to ourselves, "I ought to eat" or "I ought to stop eating now," rather than, "I feel hungry" or "I feel full."

Others of us grew up in families in which the focus was on proper nutrition, a sort of scientific approach to food and feeding. This may have meant that each meal had to be balanced with selections from the major food groups. Certain foods, especially sweets, were forbidden, and eating was confined to three meals a day. Snacking between meals was forbidden.

Other families may have been concerned with slimness for fashion or for keeping in shape. If so, sweets, fats, and carbohydrates may have been verboten and the children's weight carefully monitored.

Whatever feelings and rules your parents had in regard to food and feeding, and however these were communicated to you, you can be fairly sure that: (a) your parents believed that their approach to food was in your best interest; (b) the way feeding was handled in your home was often quite unrelated to hunger; and (c) your parents' approach has had a strong influence on the way you feed your children.

One participant in our workshops told us this story: "My mother and father fled Europe during World War II. They arrived in the United States with very little money and few skills. They both worked and managed to do well. I always remember food and eating as a big deal in our house. My mother cooked an enormous amount of food, enough for an army, although we were only four. It was important to her that food be left over; extra food was a symbol of security as well as an assurance that there would always be enough. She insisted on buying the freshest vegetables, the best cuts of meat and elegantly rich desserts. She was a stickler when it came to setting the table—everything had to match, right down to the salt and pepper shakers. There was a great deal of ceremony surrounding food and eating. And of course, mother expected us to eat everything on our plates.

"I've adopted some of my mother's ways and brought them into my own family. At least once a day I like to have the whole family sit down to a full three-course meal. My style is somewhat less formal, but meals in my home are still prepared and served nicely. My five-year-old and I are constantly battling. He often asks for a peanut butter and jelly sandwich or a bowl of cereal at mealtimes. It has been very hard for me to reconcile my upbringing with his food desires. When I'm honest with myself, I have to admit that he doesn't have the capacity to eat huge quantities of food nor can he sit through a long meal comfortably. He'd rather eat earlier when he is hungry and without the fanfare. But it is hard for me to give up the tie to my past represented by a formal dinnertime."

Many of us retain pleasant memories of family mealtimes and rituals. But what happens when we try to relive our past by sharing remembered food and eating experiences with our own children and they simply are not interested? One father described such a situation: "I always knew when it was Saturday morning because my father would be in the kitchen preparing his ritual French toast breakfast. That was the only time he ever cooked. We were four boys, and I can remember the excitement as each of us got old enough to help. We learned the secret ingredients that went into his egg mixture, just how hot to cook the oil and how thick to cut the bread slices. The toast had to be cooked to golden brown perfection. Naturally I was sure I would continue this tradition when I had my own family. Boy, was I upset when my son said to me, 'I don't like French toast, and anyhow I'd rather watch TV now.' How could he break the tradition? Didn't he understand the importance of Saturday morning breakfast?"

Fortunately this father was smart enough to realize that the Saturday breakfast ritual was not as important to his children as it had been to another generation of boys. He continued the French toast breakfast for himself, but the children ate what they wanted.

To implement the self-demand feeding approach that we talk about in this book, you will have to guard against the temptation to mold your children's eating behavior to fit traditions that have nothing to do with them.

Food as Love

As we have seen, almost from the moment of birth, food has symbolic as well as real meaning. When we were infants, food was an extension of our mother and was associated with warmth, security, touching, closeness—love. As we grew and began to experience the world around us, we learned to distinguish between mother and food, but something of that early connection between food and love was retained. For many parents, a gift of love was the food they prepared for us. One mother remembered her own mother presenting her with a special dish at dinner saying, "There's an extra helping of love in this." She in turn, made a special dish, a "love omelet" for her children.

The intertwining of food and love is seen in mothers' gestures and words in many cultures. How often have we heard mothers gently urging, "Eat, eat, my darling," *"Iss, iss, mein Kind,"* or *"Mange, mange, bambino."* Their expressions of warmth and concern often had the effect of obscuring our real physical needs. As a result, many of us never learned to distinguish food as something other than gifts from mother. This program helps you teach your children to make that distinction—to be able to love you in many ways but to eat for themselves.

Culture

Our childhood experiences have greatly affected the nature and intensity of our involvement with food, but our current culture also influences us. Magazines, newspapers, radio, television and the movies bombard us daily, promoting ideas that have nothing to do with our nutritional or physical needs.

Food fads and trends sweep across the country in a matter of weeks. We wonder if the originators of *Sesame Street* ever dreamed that a generation of adults would pick up the Cookie Monster's mania and join a nationwide chocolate-chip-cookie obsession. Ice-cream enthusiasts not only stand on long lines for their Haagen-Dazs, Baskin-Robbins or Swensen's, but even wear T-shirts advertising their favorite brand. In this country of abundance, even water has its devotees who will only drink Perrier, Poland Springs or Calistoga.

Our society also has well-established conventions and rituals around food. Can you think of any significant gathering at which food does not play a prominent role? All family events seem to demand food—from the birth of babies to birthdays, engagements, weddings, family get-togethers and even deaths. Some social activities even have become associated with specific foods. What is a sports event without a hot dog? Or a movie without popcorn? Could you conceive of having a birthday party without ice cream and cake? Or Thanksgiving minus stuffed turkey and pie?

What do these conventions have to do with individual tastes and hunger? Nothing. Every Thanksgiving, between 1:00 and 6:00 P.M., millions of Americans sit down to eat turkey. Can a whole nation be hungry for the same food on the same day and at exactly the same time? What on earth would happen if you wanted to serve lasagna for Thanksgiving, or fruit salad and almond cookies at a birthday party? The idea is scandalous.

Social Standards of Appearance

Joshua Lukas Smith
Born July 3, 1984
7 lbs. 6 oz., and 17 inches long!

The baby's body size is calculated and announced the day of his birth. In fact, parents begin thinking about size and physical attributes even before the baby is born. They say, "I hope the baby has your build and metabolism." "I hope she does not get my nose." "I hope he is tall like me." From the first viewing, parents, relatives and friends assess whom the baby resembles in its features, build and expressions. Comparisons and evaluations are constantly being made. We never hear, "Oh, my son looks just like himself!"

From the earliest moments of life we begin to judge on the basis of looks. We live in a society that puts enormous emphasis on personal appearance and sets norms that are often unreachable and unrealistic. Placing so high a priority on appearance over other personal attributes inflicts enormous harm on children. The challenge to us as parents is to allow our children to be who they are physically, without fear or humiliation—to find their own body size comfortable, though it may vary from the charts.

What does body size have to do with self-demand feeding? We are often led to impose controls on our child's eating and interfere with self-regulation because we are trying to control body size. We want our children to look a certain way, to meet an idealized standard of beauty.

When body size becomes a struggle between parent and child, there is a much greater chance of an ongoing weight problem or a distorted body image. Children's bodies change dramatically as they grow. There is no point in worrying about overweight or underweight, since the child will most likely outgrow the extremes.

We don't come off assembly lines. We are not replicas of one another nor of Madison Avenue's or Hollywood's icon of the day. We come in billions of different sizes, shapes, colors and textures—to a large extent genetically predetermined. Heredity has dictated that some of us will have greater muscular definition, be more or less hairy, have rounder or flatter bottoms, wider or narrower hips or shoulders, be flatter or bustier, and on and on.

Sadly, many of us accept the media message that there are ideal shapes for human beings and that if we fail to fit the form, we are deficient. People go to all sorts of extremes to make their bodies "correct." Women, particularly, put themselves through considerable pain and often great risk and expense trying to conform to the ideal standard. Procedures used in cosmetic surgery are given cute descriptive names to hide their severity, but *tummy tuck, nose job, face lift* are terms that hardly reveal the slicing, cutting away and rearranging of skin, flesh and bone that take place in the name of beauty. Breast reduction, cellulite removal and hair transplants are more common than ever before.

Body reshaping by exercise is also in vogue. Exercise, of course, can and should be an enjoyable and health-giving experience. But how many people put themselves through daily pain and sometimes physical risk trying desperately to get into shape? Exercise is not enjoyable for them; it's a punishment they impose on themselves for having a shape different from the current model.

Today's ideal image is to be very thin. Look at the models. Look at the mannequins in store windows. Adult clothes are shown on figures that are more and more like sticks.

In trying to remove every ounce of fat, we struggle to be what we're not and probably never can be. As a result we never feel good in our bodies. We call this a *dis-ease* with our bodies. This dis-ease is catching. It is passed from society to parent to child.

The pressures to conform to an idealized standard start at birth. What a rude awakening when you take your baby for his first checkup with the pediatrician. The infant is placed on a scale, and you are made to feel that you are on trial, that you are being weighed in. Will you pass the test? The charts are pulled out, and you are shown where your baby fits on the curve. Does your baby's growth meet the norm? If it does, you relax. What happens if your baby is in the lower 10 percent range? Must you go home and fatten him up? Does anyone explain that perhaps this is not serious underweight, but a perfectly acceptable and healthy size? If your baby is in the upper 90 percent, does this mean she is doomed to a lifelong weight problem, or does it mean that she needs to carry more weight than other babies?

A person's body should be pleasing and give pleasure *to the owner*. Just as we want our child to develop her own organic sense of her hunger, we also want her to build a positive sense of her body.

Self-image

Many of us look to our child's accomplishments to enhance our own self-worth. We push our children to achieve academically, athletically and socially to meet not their needs but ours. Not surprisingly, our sense of self can also become enmeshed with our child's appearance. We want our child to look a certain way, so *we* will be seen in a good light. Maria, the mother of four-year-old Robin, said, "It's hard for me to admit this, but I feel very embarrassed about Robin's body. She weighs fifty pounds. It's not so bad when I'm home alone with her, but when we go out, I feel terrible. People look at Robin and I'm sure that they're thinking, 'What kind of mother could have let that happen?' I even dress her in layers to try to cover the weight."

Another parent responded with, "I know what you mean. I think that when my son looks good, I look good." And then a third said, "When my six-year-old was an infant and toddler, he was always dressed impeccably. I believed that his looking so good gave a message to the world that I was a good mother."

Nancy, age forty-one, who is of normal size, watches her diet and weighs herself on a daily basis. Her concerns with her own body made her unnecessarily anxious about her daughter: "I'm so worried about my six-year-old because she's five pounds overweight, and who knows where that will lead. I've started to restrict her sweet intake and I'm trying to cook low-calorie foods for her. I know five pounds doesn't sound like much, but all my life I've been struggling with gaining and losing the same ten pounds."

As more men become involved in the feeding of their children, they, too, will have to learn to separate their relationship to food and body size from their child's needs. One father came to a workshop because he had a three-year-old son who was underweight and ate only low-calorie foods. Though the boy had no medical problems, his father had taken him to several doctors to get advice on how to help him gain weight and grow. When we began to talk, the real problem became apparent. The father was five feet four inches tall. His wife was petite. The son weighed five pounds twelve ounces at birth and had remained small for his age. If this three-year-old had been a girl, the father might have had an easier time accepting such a small, thin child, but to have his son perceived as tiny and frail was too much for him to handle.

The father described how awful it was to grow up short. Everyone had made fun of him. He felt terrible about himself as a child and didn't want his son to go through the same pain. But this father's pain was making an unnecessary food problem for his son. Who knows how tall a three-year-old will become? Will overfeeding make him taller and resolve the father's feelings about growing up short? Perhaps the boy will not feel as negative about his size as his father did. A child can be helped to be comfortable with his body size, but not by a parent overwhelmed by his own pain and perceived inadequacy.

Men are strongly influenced by the omnipresent six-foot, broad-shouldered, slim-hipped, flat-bellied models who have dominated the media for years. The fashions have changed somewhat over time, but the obsession with the right shape persists. There is enormous pressure for adolescent boys to look like the idealized male figures of the day. One forty-two-year-old father told us, "When I was growing up in the forties, the goal was to look like Charles Atlas. There was a comic-book ad that showed a skinny kid getting sand kicked in his face by the local bully. After taking the mail-order body-building course and developing a physique like Tarzan's he retaliates and pops the bully in the nose. My whole gang sent in for the course, but not a single Tarzan developed among us."

Skinny boys on the block were the butt of jokes, but the chubby ones had plenty of problems too. Many boys growing into manhood had terrible conflicts between their natural feelings of hunger and the wish to get into shape, be strong and fit into some idealized form.

The Maternal Dilemma

Women, however, have a unique relationship to food and body size. They are raised to be especially concerned with how they look and how much they eat. They are also in a particular bind when it comes to feeding children. To be a mother has traditionally meant that you provide for your children—that you feed them. Though fathers also provide for others, they have, at least in the past, done so by bringing home the bacon that mother then prepared and served.

Women are judged, by themselves as well as by others, by how well they do this job of feeding. Contemporary working women may not have their sense of self or of personal accomplishment bound up entirely in what's for dinner the way women of previous generations did; nevertheless, food and feeding still hold center stage. Mothers spend a great deal of their waking day involved in one way or another with food. While there are some men who take primary responsibility for the feeding of the family, in a large number of families the mother plans the menu, buys the food and prepares the meals.

Further complicating women's role as nurturer is the additional requirement that to be attractive to men, they must have the ideal body—and for many years that has meant *thin*. The results of our national obsession with thinness include an endless parade of diet books, fashions that suit only slim women, artificial nonfattening foods of every description, an epidemic of cosmetic surgery and, at the extreme, the deaths of young girls from anorexia and bulimia. At any given time there are 65 million people, mostly women, dieting in this country.

What must this pressure do to a woman's feelings about food? To stay thin, she must impose severe food restrictions on herself. Even though she is involved with food and feeding so much of the time, it is for others, not for her. Women see the food they prepare as pleasurable for others and dangerous for themselves. For many, food becomes the enemy. As a result, women often bring great ambivalence, perhaps even resentment to their responsibility for feeding their families. It is difficult to give freely to others while depriving yourself. In order to meet society's ideal of feminine slimness, a woman must deny her own hunger signals. How can she trust her children's hunger signals, let alone teach them to listen to their body cues about hunger and food, when she has worked so hard to avoid listening to her own?

Your Child's Self-image

Babies do not look in a mirror to assess their bodies. For years the assessment is done for them and is reflected in the mirrored glances of the parent. When this mirroring conveys the parent's negative feeling, the child's sense of her body can be damaged. Children are adept at reading their parents' feelings. One mother reported, "I hate to watch Alice, who's eight, get undressed at night. I feel repulsed by the flab on her tummy and thighs. I had a weight problem as a teenager, and now I work very hard at keeping myself thin. Alice's fat makes me crazy. I know she senses my repulsion. Already she talks very negatively about her body. She thinks she's a failure because she doesn't meet my standards."

How does parental criticism, voiced or unvoiced, affect children? When the criticism is against the child's body, it has a different impact than if it is aimed at an isolated act. For example, if a parent is upset because the child's room is a mess, this is experienced as "something I do is unacceptable to my parents." But when a parent expresses criticism of a child's body, the child feels that *he is, at his core, unacceptable.* It's not his behavior but rather who he is that is unacceptable.

One father told us of putting his five-year-old overweight daughter, Janice, on an exercise regime because her overweight was so upsetting to him. He would urge Janice to move, "Let's all go jogging!"; he would invent reasons to get her to move faster, "Run into my bedroom and get my glasses." "Instead of taking the elevator, let's take the stairs." He would find himself feeling angry and mortified in the local playground when Janice could not do what the other children could. She liked the swings, but he would encourage her to master the jungle gym, which she had trouble with and did not like. He was embarrassed with his friends because Janice was overweight. Even though Janice's father did not voice his criticism and embarrassment, the child felt it. And in rebellion, Janice began to consume larger and larger quantities of food. When they were out shopping, she would run into food stores and ask for food, much to her father's dismay. In this situation, once again, the child seemed to be measured only for her body size. She knew this, was angered by it and chose to rebel by getting even bigger.

Of course many of us carelessly go even further than the frown of disapproval and actually tell our children what we feel about what we see. *Fat, chunky, pudgy, chubby, husky* are negative appraisals that children pick up. They learn early that fat is a stigma. Studies have shown that preschool children associate being fat with being ugly, stupid, sloppy, mean, lazy and dishonest and have a preference for children who are not fat.

Even a seemingly neutral label like *big* can get equated with *fat*. One ninth-grader told us that she was always one of the tallest in her class in elementary and junior high school. She heard over and over again what a "big girl" she was and she began thinking of herself as fat. The adjective *big* applied to her through her early childhood gave her a distorted and negative body image.

Peer Pressure

When the peer group labels, teases or makes judgments about a child's body size or body parts, the pain and self-consciousness of the experience can linger forever. One mother recalled, "When I was in high school, I was a cheerleader, which was supposed to be an honor. I've always been narrow on top and broader on the bottom. When I would cheerlead in my short skirt, all the boys would yell, 'Hey, legs.' The pleasure and honor were gone. I always felt terrible about this nickname, and to this day I am very self-conscious about my legs."

Another parent reported, "Rona, a friend's nine-year-old daughter, refused to eat dinner at our house recently. When I asked her why she wasn't eating, she said, 'I'm too fat.' To me, this girl looked perfectly normal, but she explained, 'The kids my age doing modeling are much thinner than me. Also, my mom says I'm getting a little belly. At school when my friends and I get together, we talk about what we don't like about ourselves. Sally has braces and hates her teeth; Jenny wears glasses and feels bad about that; Aviva can't stand her hair, she wishes it would curl. Anyway, I didn't know what to say, so I just started to say I was fat'."

The sad part of this story is that these young girls would never think of talking about what they like about their bodies, and Rona felt she *had* to pick a negative trait.

Am I What I Weigh?

Children pick up society's message about body size and weight and feel they must conform. Diane, age sixteen, told us, "My brother was getting married last February. There were going to be lots of people there who hadn't seen me in years. I wanted to be *noticed*, so I decided in June to start losing weight. I began by doing Jane Fonda exercises every day and dieting. I managed to stick to it until the wedding—eight months! I lost ten inches and lots of pounds. I went to the wedding, read a prayer, and gave a very funny speech that I wrote myself. I was really outgoing and social, not moody and withdrawn like I often am. I looked fabulous; everyone told me so. *And I was noticed.*"

We asked Diane if she was noticed because she wrote and delivered such a wonderful speech in addition to making an attempt to reach out to the guests? "Oh, no, never!" was her response. "It was because *I looked good!*"

One fifteen-year-old, Brenda, described a date she had two weeks before. She said the boy never called again. "Why do you suppose that is?" we asked. She replied, "If only I were ten pounds thinner or if I had dressed a bit differently, he would have called." She never even considered that perhaps the two of them just didn't click or that perhaps the boy wasn't worth her time if he was so superficial and only interested in looks.

Mark was a natural comedian and storyteller with a great facility for making his friends laugh. He had a wide and varied circle of friends, both boys and girls. Mark was also quite overweight. We asked him how he came to be such a wonderful raconteur, and somewhat sadly he told us that he had developed this art in order to be liked and accepted. He thought that the kids wouldn't like him otherwise because he was overweight.

Mark was quick-witted and articulate from an early age. Fat or thin, this boy is going to be loved and accepted because of who he is, yet he believes that he is defined by his weight and that his skills are merely compensation for the weight problem. The girls, too, vastly overestimated the role their weight played in the events they described. Children, like many adults, tend to give to weight a power that it really doesn't have, and in many cases, this can be paralyzing. The belief that who you are or what you can be is ordained by body size leaves little room for self-definition through personal action and achievement.

. . .

How can we end this rampant *dis-ease* that has afflicted both children and adults? We can start by helping our children accept and feel at ease in their bodies. As difficult as this may be, we must, as parents, watch for the subtle ways in which we promote the "perfect" body notion. Too much parental interference with and commentary about a child's body inhibits her from developing her *own* sense of her body. The child must grow to understand and appreciate her body and be able to trust the many important signals the body sends. When parents rigidly enforce feeding schedules, exercise regimes, even clothing requirements, a question is raised about whom the child's body belongs to.

Children should think about their bodies in positive terms. One mother told us, "I overheard my twelve-year-old telling her four-year-old sister that she has a fat tummy. I walked over and said, 'No, her tummy is just right for her. Some of us have bodies that go out more than others. All people are built differently. Some are tall and others short; some wide, others narrow; some have rough skin, others smooth.'" This mother had exactly the right idea. Children should know that everyone has unique physical characteristics, and they need not be viewed negatively. Children can get to know their bodies and to experience pleasure in their bodies. Let's stop the assembly-line packaging and enjoy the variety!

II

FROM
YEAR TO YEAR

The next few chapters show you how to implement self-demand feeding *at whatever age your child is now.* It is important to say from the start that no child can be pigeonholed—that's why attunement is such an essential ingredient to self-demand feeding. What your child can do at two, another may do at three. You will need to adjust this program to your child's readiness for what we describe. Obviously what is important is the method and its application, not the chronological age when it occurs.

9

THE FIRST
YEAR OF LIFE

The Hospital

Although there have been revolutionary developments in certain areas of maternal-infant care, some of the concerns of parents may not be shared by the hospital where the baby is born. Most parents want to begin immediately to shape the experience of their newborn, but hospital regulations and staff schedules may come between you and your infant. To find out what to expect and how best to deal with the particular state of affairs, it can be helpful to talk with your doctor or midwife before the delivery.

If you have decided to feed your baby on demand, discuss with the doctor the need to start this approach as quickly as possible. If there is rooming-in, you may be able to begin immediately feeding your infant when she is hungry and discover the rhythm and schedules that come naturally to you both.

You may not be able to overturn hospital procedures, but parents can exercise some control. For example, you can ask the nursery staff not to give your baby a bottle of water as a substitute for a feeding. You can reinforce this by asking your doctor or midwife to write these instructions in red on your chart. You can try to urge the nurses to bring your baby to you if she is crying. Be brave and remember that once you are home, you'll be in a much better position to focus on what your infant needs and wants. Don't worry if these first few days aren't smooth sailing. It will take time to adjust to this new addition to your life.

Not Every Cry Is for Food

Needless to say, not every cry is caused by the baby's hunger. Yet many parents fall into the habit of responding automatically with food, often because of their understandable desire to cut off the noise. All of us have felt annoyed, panicked and confused by our infant's wailing. In public, we were sure that the looks in our direction were accusing us of child neglect, if not abuse. No wonder we were quick to reach for the baby's bottle. At these times it is hard to hold back and try to figure out what the crying is really about. But it is essential that we try to develop the patience and fortitude to do this.

How *do* you determine what the crying is about? If you have just fed your baby and in a few minutes she is crying again, you may want to check her diaper. If that doesn't do it, maybe she has gas and needs to burp. Sometimes your baby's cry will mean, "I'm too warm, undress me," or, "I'm too cold, please add another blanket." If you pick her up and the crying stops, then she has told you she needed a change in position or physical contact with you. The cry could mean, "I'm bored. Walk me, bounce me on your knee, turn on my mobile, hang a picture over my crib, take me into another room, sing me a song." Of course, even if she has just eaten, her cry may mean, "I'm hungry for more."

Crying is the way an infant signals distress. Although figuring out your baby's signals may seem like trying to decipher Morse code, don't give up. Some days will be better than others. As you read the cues and respond appropriately, the baby will feel both reassured and satisfied. Remember, she does not necessarily want to eat every time she cries. Remember also that your attuned responses to her varying needs help her to begin to discriminate one sensation from another. As she grows, she will learn that hunger is satisfied by food, tiredness by sleep, boredom by activity.

Sucking Needs

Babies enter this world all mouth. They need and love to suck. *The trick is to tell the difference between your infant's need to suck and his need to be fed—which also involves sucking.* It is tempting to use food as the pacifier, but if you do that, sucking gets mixed up with hunger for the infant. The message you are probably transmitting is that food meets all needs. If you give your infant a pacifier or let him suck on your finger when he needs food, he will turn away or spit it out; but if the need is for sucking, he will be content.

Holding Versus Feeding

"When Neil was an infant, I loved the warmth and closeness of breast-feeding and I was pleased that I could take my baby anywhere without having to worry about bottles and formulas. A pattern developed where each time Neil seemed upset, I would let him nurse. My response was very automatic. I offered the breast without knowing exactly what was troubling him. When I began trying to wean him, he was inconsolable. I tried rocking him and holding him, but only nursing would calm him down. I realized I shouldn't have relied only on nursing to comfort him."

"When Johanna was six months old, I returned to work and I was so glad to find a progressive day care center. I liked their policy that any baby who wanted a bottle had to be held by one of the workers. Unfortunately this policy extended to toddlers as well. At three, Johanna showed no interest in giving up her bottle and at home insisted that one of us hold her while she drank."

The day care center policy had caused Johanna to equate feeding with being held. Johanna had not learned to soothe herself and was using the bottle to keep up the physical contact with the feeder. She was not using it primarily to meet her hunger needs.

Since infants are usually held while they're fed, a baby may accept the bottle or breast without being hungry because he wants and needs skin contact, warmth and attention.

We would caution parents to try to avoid using the breast or bottle to meet all of the infant's emotional needs. From the beginning, use a range of other measures to soothe your baby. Babies like being sung to, carried, rocked, played with, talked to, shown things, caressed and held. The breast and bottle should be offered only when the baby is hungry.

Breast Versus Bottle

Self-demand feeding begins with either milk or formula from breast or bottle. We encourage mothers to read the literature on the merits and advantages of breast feeding (see Suggested Readings). Our focus, however, is not on which method to choose but rather on feeding issues that will emerge with either method.

It is crucial that you find a feeding method that suits you. Whether you choose bottle or breast, consistency with your life-style is most important so that you will feel comfortable and positive when you feed your child. This ease will be communicated to your baby, and the feeding experience will be most satisfying to you both. If you are not attuned to your own needs, you may begin to resent the baby as well as the whole feeding process. Sometimes it can be difficult to make a choice because of current cultural biases. Just remember that not everyone is the same and that there is no one "correct" choice.

You may decide to breast-feed and quickly find out that what has been labeled "natural" is not that easy after all. Your infant's sucking starts your milk production, but it can take weeks before the supply is regulated. Even when all is going as it should, there are times when your breasts hurt, either because your baby skips a feeding and the breasts become engorged or because the baby's sucking hurts your nipples. You may wonder what is so natural about someone sucking at your nipples for an extended amount of time? You are fatigued, unsure and worried at the same time. You're also overjoyed and amazed. The baby is just as unsure of its new environment. At the start, the feeding relationship is anything but natural. It will take time for both of you to get in synch with each other.

Breast-feeding mothers often wonder if the baby is actually getting enough to eat and if they are producing enough milk. One mother told this story: "I was very excited about breast-feeding Ted. Yet, it looked like I didn't have enough milk! I was devastated when my doctor told me that Ted wasn't gaining enough weight. Naturally I felt I was to blame. It was me— my body—which couldn't do what comes naturally to most women. I felt that my body had failed me and, of course, him."

If a baby needs supplemental bottles or if breast-feeding does not work, don't worry. There is much more to mothering than your milk supply. Your ability to respond with the food he needs when he is hungry, in whatever form that takes, is what is important.

The question "How much does my baby need?" is always on parents' minds. When you breast-feed, you can never really know how much your baby is getting at a particular feeding. Some babies nurse frequently, taking small portions each time. Other babies go long intervals between feedings and may consume a lot each time. Moreover, individual babies change their habits of eating. A baby's desire for food may be affected by temperament, a cold, distractions, fatigue, and so forth. The baby's capacity for food also changes as she grows. Babies frequently have growth spurts during which food consumption may increase. When the growth levels off, so does the eating. Remember, growth is uneven. Most development occurs with three steps forward, two steps back and then forward again. For many of us who "need to know," it can be difficult to go with the flow! Trust your infant. She knows when she is hungry and when she is full. As the world-renowned baby doctor, Dr. Benjamin Spock, says, "A baby knows a lot about diet. She is the one who knows how many calories her body needs and what her digestion can handle."

Parents who bottle-feed have a slightly different dilemma. You know how much is being taken at each feeding, but there is a strong temptation to assume that some measured amount, four ounces, six ounces, twelve ounces, is what your baby *should* drink. You worry that if the infant doesn't take that amount, she is not getting enough. Conversely, some parents worry that if their baby drinks more than the customary amount, she is being overfed.

Remember that the infant is capable of being self-regulating, of turning away when full, of expressing discomfort when there has not been enough. Trust that with self-demand feeding she will grow at her own pace. Dr. Donald Winnicott, a leading British pediatrician and psychoanalyst, wrote, "If the relationship between mother and baby has started and is developing naturally, then there is no need for feeding techniques, and weighings and all sorts of investigations; the two together know what is just right better than any outsider ever can. In such circumstances an infant will take the right amount of milk at the right speed, and will know when to stop."

Try to avoid thinking in ounces. Feed your baby until he lets you know he is full. His signal to you can take many forms: turning away from the bottle, pushing it away, spitting up, falling asleep, looking content. Sometimes he'll need to burp but then wish to resume drinking. Get to know his signals. And remember that the need varies from baby to baby and from feeding to feeding.

One mother told us of a device she used: "Each time I feed Angie, even when I know that she'll only take a few ounces, I fill up an eight-ounce bottle. I always offer her double what I think she'll take. This way I avoid thinking that the right amount for her is the amount in the bottle and I simply let her drink until she lets me know she is full."

Solid Foods

An exciting event is about to happen. Your infant is ready to eat solid foods, and that marks a change in the relationship between parents and child. For fathers whose babies have been breast-fed, it is the opportunity to become involved in feeding. For both parents, the change invariably brings with it a host of questions: What kind of food should I start with? How much should I give him? When? What temperature should the foods be? Can I continue to allow the baby to have significant control over his eating?

Most pediatricians will offer a suggested food list to begin with. Frequently, cereals, rice, mashed vegetables, bananas and other mashed fruits are on the list. All parents have stories to tell about their child's first eating experience. "I was looking forward to giving Harry solid food because it meant that I wouldn't have to be the sole provider anymore. I bought what was called in my childhood baby pablum, and when I gave it to him, the baby looked at me with disgust and spit it all out. Friends told me to keep trying, that the problem was just that pablum was new to him. It took me a long time to realize that maybe he didn't like the taste. What a surprise, because my mother and generations of mothers before her had started with this cereal. Finally, I decided to try something else. Would you believe that strained carrots were a hit?"

Even little babies have discriminating tastes. As parents we should, from the beginning, try to respond to their likes and dislikes. Offer a variety of foods to your infant. The food lists your doctor gives you may be a source of comfort—he's the "expert"—but the real experts are you and your child. Schedules and lists limit your spontaneity and creativity in food selection and your ability to find and respond to the particular tastes of your child. What may sound like a rather unusual example makes our point: "At eleven months of age we took our son to a Chinese restaurant. I brought with me a jar of baby food, but it became clear that he was more interested in the sesame noodles. He seemed to enjoy the way the noodles slipped through his tiny fingers, stuck on his head and even slipped down his throat. He ate, and still eats, a lot of sesame noodles."

Another question we hear from parents is "How do we balance food intake and milk intake?" At first your baby needs very little solid food. T. Berry Brazelton, a distinguished pediatrician and noted author, tells parents that the daily requirement in the first year of life is "a pint of milk or its equivalent —cheese, ice cream—one ounce fresh fruit juice, two ounces of iron-containing protein and a multi-vitamin is optional."

With solid food, too, your baby will give you signals. When she has had enough of the offered food, she will signal an end, probably by turning away. This may not mean that she is full, but only that she has had enough of the solid food. She may still be hungry for milk from breast or bottle.

Parents vary in how they introduce new foods. One parent told us, "I offer Lucy her milk after a few spoonfuls of the new food. This prevents her from first filling up on milk and gives me the chance to test out the new food." Another mother had a different way of handling this situation: "When Phil gets hungry, I've noticed that he becomes a bit frantic, and since I want to make eating a pleasurable experience, I first nurse him for a few minutes, just to take the edge off his hunger. Then I offer him the food and nurse afterward as well."

There is no one right way to handle the introduction of solid foods. Remember, you can take your cues from your baby. He will tell you much of what you need to know to make this a pleasurable experience for both of you.

Not all children are ready for solid food at the same time. Some parents worry when, at six months, their babies show no interest in solid foods. This should not be a cause for concern. Studies have shown that children can thrive perfectly well on milk or formula for the first year. When your baby is ready, she will eat. Starting at the point when you and your pediatrician feel it would be appropriate to begin solid foods, try different foods and see if she responds to one or more eagerly. If not, wait several days and try again. Don't push. The process may go on for several months. Often babies indicate their readiness for solid food when they reach for the foods others are eating.

Another consideration often overlooked in feeding infants, is pace. The timing of each spoonful and the amount on the spoon can affect your child's response to the feeding. If food is offered too slowly, this can be frustrating for the child. On the other hand, pushing the food too quickly can be uncomfortable and overwhelming to the baby. His turning away or spitting up may be a response to the fast pace rather than an indicator of fullness. To a large extent these problems take care of themselves when the parent pays careful attention to the child. It's like learning a new dance. If you pay close attention to the steps and the rhythm of your partner, tripping can be kept at a minimum.

After a few months of experimentation, solid food will be a part of your child's life. You will be moving slowly from spoon-feeding him foods you've selected and prepared, to his using fingers and spoon and choosing what he likes and dislikes. The mashed bananas that he gobbled down yesterday he may turn away from today. Or he may want to eat bananas most of the time. Try to relax around the foods and let him guide you. It is not important that he like or try every food you offer. These months are a testing period. You are exposing him to different foods and also to utensils—spoon, cup, plate. Just as you are not overly concerned if he turns away from a newly offered rattle, mobile or toy, you should not be troubled if he turns away from some of the new foods.

Some people worry that their infants are eating too much

and would never stop if the parents didn't exercise control. It is extremely rare that young children will actually eat beyond their hunger and take in more than they need. The seemingly large intake at a particular feeding or over some stretch of time is usually attributable to the fact that neither hunger nor growth are static. There will always be variations in the child's need for food.

As you begin to offer food to your baby, say out loud, "Are you hungry?" Even though he won't understand, the baby will begin to associate hunger pangs with food. This is good preparation for the attitude about food you're trying to achieve.

Food for Play

Babies will make a mess during feedings. Indeed, when they first begin to feed themselves, "mess" does not adequately describe the scene. The kitchen can look like a war zone where food fights have raged. The child does not yet know that food is more than a plaything. His world is explored through touch, taste and smell. He finds out about food by feeling it, squeezing it, throwing it, spitting it.

Parents, who have the thankless job of cleaning up and restoring order, are naturally reluctant to relinquish the spoon to the baby. But just as he learns about the properties of food, he will also want to learn about the nature of his eating utensils. By banging the spoon, he learns it makes noises; he sees that it can hold food and other items, that it can be moved around, and that it shines. This exploration, a consequence of improved mobility and dexterity, is age-appropriate.

Though it can be trying for you, mess making is an important developmental experience. Here are some ideas that may help: Allow a reasonable amount of food play. The mess is less if smaller amounts are available to play with. You can put clear plastic or newspaper on the high chair and the floor beneath it to catch the mess. If it becomes clear that your baby is obviously not interested in eating and you think she's had enough time playing with the food, then it is time to remove her from the high chair and give her a few toys. Or, let her remain at the table but remove the food and replace it with toys.

One father who attended our workshops shared a creative

solution to a problem he confronted: "It was Thanksgiving, and our family was invited to my boss's house for dinner. Needless to say, I was worried about my youngest child's ability to wreak havoc at this formal affair. She can hardly sit through family meals, and when she's finished, food is everywhere. I could not imagine what she would do in this situation and I was not anxious to find out. I came up with a wonderful idea. I brought along her playpen and put it next to the dining room table. She sat in the playpen, a toy in one hand and a drumstick in the other. Everyone enjoyed the evening meal."

The question of building good character and teaching table manners concerns all of us. None of us wants to see our children grow up to be sloppy and ill mannered. How do you stop the ten-month-old from grabbing the spoon of pureed vegetables and feeding his hair, ear and cheeks instead of placing the food in his mouth? Or, what do you do when his cup of milk is tipped over on his lap and begins to dribble on the floor? Should he be reprimanded? The answer is a definite no! The child at this developmental level is just learning how to hold a spoon and cup. He can't really feed himself, but he has to be given the opportunity to practice. That's how he will learn. You should gently assist him in holding the utensils properly and help guide his hand, or better yet, have two spoons and plates—yours for feeding and teaching by example, and his for experimentation.

10

GROWING UP AND OUT: AGES ONE THROUGH FOUR

Parents who have been using the self-demand feeding method or who now introduce it will find these next four years particularly rewarding. If you can keep the goals clearly in mind and let them guide you, the seas ahead will be sailed fairly smoothly. Self-demand feeding will encourage personal growth and independence. The child's relationship to food will develop in a way that fosters eating enjoyment and natural self-regulation while causing minimal stress. Let's review the main points:

- Your child is able to tell you *when* she's hungry.
- She can tell you *what* she wants to eat.
- She knows *how much* she needs; she can stop when full.

Many issues will come up as you implement this approach. We will address these issues according to the age group in which they're most likely to occur. Don't be alarmed if your child is displaying a certain behavior at a different age. Each child has his or her own time clock.

Twelve to Twenty-four Months

FOOD PLAY

The mess making that started at the end of your baby's first year will continue at full tilt into his second year. He still needs to explore his food and play with it. We have heard of many instances where young children of this age go on hunger strikes, at least against solid foods, and the parents can't understand why. When we've asked the parents to describe what precipitated the problem, it usually had to do with not allowing the child to mess and play with the food. Prematurely stopping the baby's exploration of food may be setting the stage for future difficulties. Eating should be pleasurable. Much of that pleasure for the one-year-old comes from playing with food, smearing it, dropping it and touching it to various parts of the body—hair, ears, nose, chin, cheek. You've probably noticed how upset he gets when you try to clean him up. He wants to wear his food until *he* is ready to relinquish it to the washcloth. He likes tearing his bagel apart, making crumbs out of toast, using applesauce as finger paint, holding the spoon and banging it against his plate and high chair. He often prefers all this to eating. Many parents get very worried when their child's food intake appears to be sacrificed to his food games.

Frances, the mother of a one-year-old, told us, "It can be terribly frustrating feeding Helaine. First of all, the time involved is overwhelming. When she was an infant, I could feed her in fifteen minutes with a minimum of mess and fuss. Now it might take me forty-five minutes on a good day. The problem is that she not only wants to play while being fed, she also wants to do more of the feeding herself. She forgets that she is supposed to be eating, she gets so involved with the mess making. Then I worry that she hasn't gotten enough to eat. When she's finished, I have to give her a bath to get her clean; then I have to clean her high chair, the floor around her, sometimes the walls, her clothes and bib and, at times, even I need a shower. I'm pooped when I'm finished."

We understand that most parents can't spend that much time whenever a child wants to eat. Since we've stressed the importance of allowing a child of this age to play and mess, how can parents accommodate their own needs with that of their child's? The only way is to make certain compromises. Not every meal has to be for play. You can decide that at least once a day, preferably a time when you're most relaxed and have time to spare, you will give your child the time she needs both to play and to eat. At other times, you will respond to her hunger but take more control of the situation by offering foods that are less messy and easier to handle, giving her an empty spoon in one hand to play with while you manage the spoon that holds the food.

FOOD INTAKE

At this age not all lack of interest in food is connected with food play. "Ray was a wonderful eater until, at about sixteen months, something happened. His appetite dwindled to nothing. He seemed so distracted at mealtimes. I became very worried that he would not eat enough. So I tried every game I knew to get him to eat. It was very hard for me to sit by patiently and watch him go from a big eater to a nibbler and picker. I began to think that he would never eat normal amounts again."

Ray's mother did not have to be so concerned. What was normal for Ray in the first year of his life is not what is normal at sixteen months. Keep in mind that your baby will never again grow at the rate he did in the first twelve months of his life. Most babies double their birth weight by four or five months and triple it by the end of the first year. Then growth slows down, and the body uses stored baby fat. The child's diminished interest in eating the food you offer and his smaller appetite are quite normal. Children are also more distracted by the environment, more involved with the outside world and with forming their own identity.

Most parents are tempted, when they see their child "losing his appetite," to try to coax him along. They fear that this disinterest in eating will stay with him forever. Over and over again we've seen that when no issue is made of his eating, the child will be able to go through this stage—however long it takes—and eat just what he needs for his growing body. Keep in mind that he is perfectly capable of being self-regulatory.

The amount of food that parents believe is necessary for their child's healthy growth is often more than a child really needs or can handle. At this age your child's lower food intake should not be met by a great deal of pressure or cajoling to encourage eating. This will only cause distress and confusion. Allow the child to find his own appropriate level of food intake, even if it looks too meager to you.

What the child eats every day may be affected by the frequency of feedings. Little children don't have the capacity to eat big meals. They may be unable, on a three-meal-a-day schedule, to consume the amount they would take if fed frequently throughout the day. Some parents who have complained that their children did not eat enough at breakfast, lunch and dinner, found that the total intake was greater when numerous small feedings were allowed, *on demand*. A child who is offered only three meals a day would be forced to consume larger quantities of food at one time. Not only is this physically impossible for a toddler, but it is totally unnecessary. Toddlers are actively exploring the world and need to refuel many times. That is why they prefer snacking on small amounts throughout the day. Allowing them to do this will also put an end to a lot of waste and unhappiness. Your child can signal hunger as she feels it during the day. Feed her when she asks to be fed.

COMMON CONCERNS

•Weaning is a very troublesome question for most parents. Please see the section on page 100.

•Your one-year-old may want to stand in her high chair while eating. Let her. Young children have a hard time sitting still, especially as they begin to walk. It won't hurt to let her stand and eat finger foods. Put one side of the high chair next to the wall with you sitting on the other side if you're afraid she will fall.

•He's teething and cranky and shows less interest in food. Offer him zwieback, a breadstick, a cracker or a frozen bagel cut into manageable pieces. A frozen bagel will nourish and soothe at the same time. It is not a good idea to offer new foods when a child is teething and has aching gums and a sore mouth.

•He is grabby, constantly reaching for your food or anyone else's, in the same way that he grabs for the phone, your wallet, your keys or anything else you own. He does not yet realize that food is just for eating. Hand him a little food—he will probably play with it and, like the keys, drop it eventually.

•He throws a tantrum when you're out on the streets if he sees someone eating or because he's really hungry. He may not be able to go very long between feedings, though you can't always interrupt your agenda to go to a restaurant or food store. Be sure to bring snack foods or a bottle wherever you go to avoid scenes and ensure feeding on demand.

•When a child has an ear infection, temperature, cold, flu or other illness, there is usually a marked disinterest in food. There may even be some weight loss. It is sad to see your child pale, sick and perhaps looking gaunt. As soon as the child is on the mend, parents naturally want to get food and liquids down him quickly and abundantly—to fatten him up. Frequently, the additional food is refused. Don't worry. Remember how repulsed you were by the sight and smell of food during and just after your last illness. Also remember that, as your energy returned, you began slowly to regain an interest in food. Trust that this will happen with your child as well. Let him ease back into normal eating. Overwhelming him with food may have the opposite result of what you desire.

REMEMBERING THE THREE BIG QUESTIONS: WHEN, WHAT, HOW MUCH?

If your child has been allowed to eat on demand since birth, nothing has changed in the food arena, even though he is making great changes every day. Your attitude during this second year is very important. Remember that he knows when he is hungry; he knows what he wants to eat; and he knows enough to stop when full. There is a temptation to begin to regulate a child as he grows older. Try to resist it and trust that he can continue along the path of self-regulation without any interference from grown-ups.

If you are beginning the self-demand feeding approach with your one-year-old, you should be asking the question "Are you hungry?" before you begin to feed him. Though he is at an age when he has some understanding of words, the question is asked just as much for your benefit as it is for his. You need to be reminded that food is a match for hunger. Your one-year-old will pick up quickly on your new attitude toward his eating.

You can place a variety of foods in front of him and let him choose, or if that seems too overwhelming for your child, try one food at a time. Again, don't be alarmed when he plays more than he eats. On the other hand, if your child eats a lot, give him enough so that he can signal when he is full. His fullness and not an empty plate should determine when the feeding is over. If he is eating a lot, it is because *his body* needs that amount.

Try to keep track of what his favorite foods are and give him those. If he turns away from a particular food, don't serve it again for a few days. If he continues to say no to it, just take it off your list of what to feed him, at least for the time being.

Your toddler is capable of telling you she's had enough. These signs can take the following form: throwing food on the floor, excessive play, sleepiness, crankiness, turning away. She will tell you if she is still hungry, be assured of that. As you remove the food from her, say, "I guess you're full now" or "I'm going to clean up now that I see you aren't hungry anymore." By speaking in these terms, she can begin to associate stopping with fullness. That way, she'll realize that fullness emanates from within herself and is the signal of when eating should stop.

Particularly during this year be sure to carry food at all times. A child of this age may get hungry while you are away from the kitchen. Be prepared.

Ages Two, Three and Four

The big word in the two-year-old's vocabulary is *no.* A major phrase is *I won't.* An endless repetition of *no* is anything but music to parents' ears, but it is the sound they're going to hear. This "no" stage may come anytime from two years old on, and it may have repercussions in the eating arena. Try to keep the ensuing battles away from the feeding situation. The "no" stage is one way your child begins to separate from you, the beginning of mastery and self-control.

At two years, your child has begun to talk, walk, point, and indicate fairly clearly her needs, likes, and dislikes. Before you place food in front of a two-year-old, ask "Are you hungry?" Why bother preparing food if the answer is no? Many times we hear exasperated parents say, "I asked Leah if she wanted eggs or toast or even pancakes, and all I got was no. Then I said, 'What do you want?' and she turned to reach for a toy." Before you ask the *what* question, you must explore the *when* question. There's no use talking about different kinds of food to a child who isn't even hungry. It may be hard to keep the question of hunger in mind, since we are all so programmed to put food on the table according to clocks rather than in response to expressions of hunger. But the three-meal-a-day approach, or any other fixed schedule you may be using, must give way to feeding based upon *hunger demands*. As we have said, in the long run this will turn out to make the feeding of your children much easier and not, as you may fear, the other way around.

Children from two through four can be very specific about their likes and dislikes. Expect to hear, in strong terms, what they want to eat, both what they "love" and what they "hate." *Yuk, echh,* and *phooey* give emphasis to youngsters' expressions of distaste.

This is also a time when a host of food-related idiosyncrasies may arise. Some children don't like their foods to touch on the plate; others only like certain colors, forms or consistency. One parent told us, "Ceci pointed to the egg salad I made her and said she wouldn't eat it because it had dirt in it. The dirt was a little pepper. That was the beginning of her spice-rejection era." This parent went on to say that her son, Jed, won't eat any soup because one day she made a bean soup and its smell offended him. Some children will only eat with a particular spoon or from a special cup or plate. Pay attention to these details because it will make your life easier and the children happier.

This is also a prime time for food jags. Your child may hit upon three or four favorite foods and not eat anything else. Before you get excited about what seems like unorthodox eating, evaluate what your child is eating over a two-week period. You will probably see that nutritional intake is more than adequate. The best check is the health of your child. If she is active, alert and apparently healthy, she is probably getting everything she needs. If you're really concerned about a particular nutritional deficit, give her a vitamin supplement. Above all, don't try to force the child to eat foods she doesn't want to eat.

WEANING

When the child becomes a toddler and begins walking and talking, there is great excitement in the air. The child will be delighted with his newfound mobility. We may find it is a big job to keep an eye on and to handle this new walker, but we also begin to see the road to some freedom from the total physical dependence. The clinging of babyhood gives way to the greater independence of childhood. But . . . not so simply. Our two-year-old runs away but then returns to our lap just as quickly.

Sometimes both mother and child are ready for weaning at the same time; then the child is readily eased off breast or bottle. Most often, though, giving up the bottle or breast is a process that brings with it some degree of stress for both parent and child. This change in the method of feeding represents a significant break with babyhood and a move toward more independence.

You may have a child who is reluctant to wean. Nursing at the breast or taking a bottle may be her final hold on her infancy and her very close attachment to you. In this society babies are weaned from the breast more quickly than they are from the bottle. Though some babies go to the bottle as a transition, many breast-fed babies go straight to the cup. Yet we have known children who were still using a bottle at age four or five.

The one-year-old still likes to suck and is still exploring the world via his mouth. This is evidenced by the number of toys and books that he gums to death. The bottle can be a source of nourishment both physically and psychologically. We would urge you not to wean a child before some readiness is shown. Some indications are: playing with breast or bottle rather than sucking; turning away from bottle or breast more frequently; shorter periods of sucking, which result in a cutting back until, eventually, the baby is interested in bottle or breast at naptime or bedtime only. No harm is done if the child progresses in all areas of his life and still falls back on a bottle. He will give it up in due time, particularly when he sees other children his age without it. If the child needs to hold on to a bottle, let him. On the other hand, you don't have to take a completely laissez-faire stance. A child who shows readiness should be encouraged in the direction of weaning. But try to be sure that encouragement—not pushing—is the dynamic. The decision should be your child's.

Alexandra, the mother of a two-year-old, said, "I couldn't stand the sight of that bottle anymore. I watched this active, bright, son of mine reach for his bottle and I felt embarrassed, ashamed, as if I were to blame."

What is all this pressure to get children grown up? Why should this mother feel so guilty if her two-year-old or even three-year-old chooses a bottle over a cup? Every child regresses in one way or another at this time. This is the way he keeps one hand in the security and familiarity of the past while the other hand is moving out in new exploration. The little steps back are in the service of his forward thrust. For one child the regressive pull may be to hold on to or return to bottle or breast, for another child it may be lapsing back into crawling, baby talk, bedwetting or other infantile behavior. If this conduct is correctly understood, it shouldn't be a source of embarrassment. The child should never be chastised or forcibly pushed forward until he's ready.

At some point you may want to help the weaning process along. Gentle nudging is fine, particularly when the child starts to show signs of readiness. But no sledgehammer approaches, please! One mother told us her solution, "At three and a half my daughter was still using her bottle and pacifier at home. When we took her for a dental appointment, I asked the dentist to tell her, without applying any pressure, that it was time to give them both up because they weren't necessary for her anymore. I wasn't in the room when he talked to her, but when we got home, she asked me to give her a bag. She put all her bottles and pacifiers in the bag and asked me to bring it over to her newborn cousin's house."

The dentist had simply told the child that she was now old enough and grown up enough to give up her pacifier and bottle. Sometimes a child can respond more easily to an outside, neutral person who is free from the tension and struggle involved in these issues.

Another parent had a different solution to the question of weaning: "I decided to involve Patrick in this weaning question. I sat him down and asked him when he thought he would like to give up his bottles. He thought for a moment and then said, 'On my third birthday before the party.' I thought it would be helpful if the finale was ceremonialized in some way, so I suggested that on that day we would gather up all the bottles and throw them in the town garbage dump. That is exactly what we did, and he never asked for a bottle from that day forward."

It's a good idea to involve the child in the decision-making process if at all possible. (Obviously, if you're weaning a pre-verbal child from the breast, there won't be a two-way discussion on the subject.) This involvement gives the child a feeling of control over his own life in addition to making him feel more responsible and committed to the decision.

Parental attitudes about weaning have a big influence on how the process goes. There are some parents who can't wait for it to happen and others who dread its arrival. Of course this has an influence on how things will turn out. Eleanor told us that even though her eighteen-month-old played at her breast more than he suckled, she couldn't bear the thought of weaning him. She encouraged him to continue to nurse because she loved the physical closeness and the special quiet time they had together. We suggested that she find a special time in the day quite separate from feeding times when she and her son could be alone. At the same time we urged her to allow the weaning process to move ahead.

Sharon was a mother who needed to rush the weaning of her one-year-old because she had just found a job. Little Sandy reacted strongly to the pressure. She screamed and screamed, refused substitute bottles and had a very hard time giving up the breast. If at all possible, wean slowly. It is preferable to wean when a child shows some readiness, but if that is not possible, as in Sharon's case, don't take the breast away abruptly. Try to do it over at least a few-weeks' span.

EXPERIMENTATION

"I don't care if Melissa and Nora don't eat all of what I offer them. I just want them to try the new food so that they can decide if they like it or not. It drives me nuts when they turn away without giving something new a chance."

"The other day I chased my four-year-old around the house with a grape in my hand. I felt like such a fool, but I knew he would like it if only I could get him to taste it, just once."

Our ideas of experimentation and our children's are two different matters. They would rather see how bread dissolves in juice than taste the wonders this world has to offer. And naturally so! We must ask ourselves why we feel it is so important that children taste everything. If children had their way, they would taste very few things and for the first few years eat a rather narrow range of foods. So what? Why is it necessary to impose our tastes on our children—and why rush them to expand their menu? Without your pushing, as they grow older, they will try most of the things you eat because children do want to emulate their parents. But they need to do it at their own pace. Remember that in the not-too-distant past there was less choice in food than we have today, and people survived very well. Offer foods but don't push them on your child. When they are ready, they will begin to experiment with new food tastes. Your child may feel safe eating the same foods each day. Allow her that.

HUNGER, FOOD SELECTION, FULLNESS

If your child is being raised with this approach, she will know when she is hungry. Parents need to remind themselves of this fact and be careful not to introduce artificial rules about eating that will interfere with the natural ability to self-regulate. To help a child from the ages of two through four develop an inner awareness of hunger, make appropriate food selections and determine when she is full, we suggest the following: (a) If your child is not expressing an interest in food or otherwise indicating hunger, *don't offer food;* (b) Begin to ask "Are you hungry?" in many different ways. Is your tummy hungry? Are you saying you're hungry because Jessica is eating or because you saw doughnuts in the bakery window? You can sit with

Jessica now while she eats and eat later when you feel hungry. We can buy you a doughnut and hold it until you get hungry. You don't have to eat it now. It won't go away. We can save it until your tummy says it's hungry.

Maria noticed that whenever three-year-old Tony was upset, he would ask for a cream cheese sandwich. One morning after having eaten he got up from the table and went to her and said, "Could you make me a sandwich?" She said, "Are you still hungry or do you want a hug instead?" He chose the hug. Each time he would request food after eating, she would repeat this question until one day Tony came to her and said, "Momma, I need a hug." With Maria's help Tony was able to understand the difference between feeding physical hunger with food and feeding emotional hunger with hugs and support.

When children feel hungry, they sometimes reach for the food that is closest or most available, though it may not be what they really want. If your child indicates hunger—perhaps by reaching for the cracker or the cookie on the counter—you may want to remind her of the available selections. "If you're hungry we also have fruit, yogurt and tuna. What would you like to eat?" Sometimes children are hungry for one food but are worried about having to give up some other choice. Alex frequently asked for a cookie when he was hungry. His mother gave him the cookie while telling him what other foods he could have. Most of the time, Alex simply held the cookie while he ate his cereal or eggs. By allowing Alex to possess the cookie, his mother gave him the necessary freedom to think about what he was really hungry for.

Now is the time to set up the children's food shelves. Room permitting, each child should have his own shelf, which *no one else can touch.* Before you go shopping, ask the children for food requests and be sure to honor them. Buy a quantity large enough so that they know that the supply won't run out immediately.

When they're hungry, they can choose something from their food shelves or eat what you've prepared. If you're just starting out with this method, you can expect your two- through four-year-old to ask for many of the heretofore "forbidden goodies." As we explained in chapters three and four, it is essential that you legalize these foods—particularly sweets. Your child may go through a period of binging until (a) the foods lose their specialness; and (b) he feels secure that they will always be available. From our observations of children who have their own food shelves in pantry and refrigerator, a pattern emerges. Although cookies and other sweets are predominant at first, within a short time the shelves become filled with a variety of foods. Peanut butter, apples, carrots, raisins, crackers and cheese are among the most common favorites, along with ice cream, cookies and gum.

Keep in mind that appetite fluctuates greatly during these years. Your child may eat a lot for a few days or weeks and then slow down to next to nothing. The swings are normal; there's no need for alarm.

Now is the time to introduce the notion of fullness. Your child knows that she can eat when hungry and choose foods that she wants. In order for her to trust that she can stop when she's full, she needs to know that the food will still be there for her when she wants it. The way to do this is by saying, "If you're full, we can wrap up the sandwich in case you get hungry for more later." Or "Let's wrap this up and write your name on it so that no one else eats it by mistake." The important thing is that she knows she can stop at any point and the food will be there when she is hungry again. She won't miss out if she stops when she's full.

We can't overemphasize the importance of assuring your child that she need not eat just because she sees the food or because she thinks this is her only opportunity to have it. As adults we are all familiar with this syndrome: who has not gone to a restaurant, ordered a special dish and felt compelled to eat far beyond fullness because "it was there?" If we allowed ourselves to take home the leftovers or reminded ourselves that we could reorder this dish some other time, the compulsion to overeat would be very much diminished. It is the same with our children.

Because of unending battles and discussions, Jeff, the father of four children from eighteen months to six years, decided to try the self-demand feeding method. He had been preparing "regular" meals—a fixed menu on a fixed schedule. There was always some child who raised a fuss about what was served or not served, what was too hot or too cold, whether there was too much sauce or too little. His wife, Diane, was skeptical, but since Jeff was the prime caretaker for the children, she let him proceed.

Jeff began by bringing the children together for a family

meeting to talk about trying an experiment. He wanted them to think about when their stomachs felt empty and then to be responsible for getting the food to fill them. He labeled the bottom shelf in the refrigerator and a low shelf in the food closet the Kids' Shelf. Using plastic containers that would ensure freshness and that the little ones could open and close easily, he filled the shelves with their favorite foods: cut-up vegetables in one, cheese slices in another, bread in another, tuna, cold chicken, peanut butter, honey and cookies. In the freezer there was plenty of ice cream. He even bought child-size plastic pitchers and filled one with juice and the other with milk. For the eighteen-month-old baby, he put prepared bottles on the refrigerator shelf.

The children were now set up to eat on demand. The three-year-old frequently took a slice of whole wheat bread and honey to make himself a sandwich. The six-year-old often helped himself to chicken and tuna. Each child, except the baby, could get his own food, pour his drinks and feed himself. Naturally the baby needed help, but the family was surprised at how little—and there was always an older child around to assist. Jeff found that food requests and nagging during the day practically disappeared. They only resurfaced when supplies ran out or when a child demanded an addition to the food list. He realized that he had to work out a system with the children whereby they would tell him when the supply was running low, before it was all gone.

Jeff, who loved to cook, still made a traditional family meal each evening. He found that most of the children were hungry for at least one item from those being served. But even if they weren't, there was no reason for concern, since they could always go to the Kids' Shelf and eat when they were hungry.

Diane's reaction to all this was quite revealing. Even though she previously hated the constant nagging and pulling at her, she now missed her involvement with the children on food issues. She had never before realized how much of her definition as a mother, provider and caretaker was wrapped up in feeding her children. Now that they were so self-sufficient with food, she felt put out to pasture. She had to rethink her role as mother.

Jeff, on the other hand, was thrilled about his children's independence and ability to take care of a most basic need. He now had more time and energy to relate to his children about other things.

Jeff, who was on the board of the neighborhood day care center his children attended, decided there was a lesson from this experiment that could be useful at the center. Now that he recognized that his children did not get hungry at the same time for the same foods, he began to think about the ritualized eating patterns at the center. Like most child-care institutions, a snack was served in the morning and again in the afternoon. Some children arrived at school having just eaten a huge breakfast, and others hadn't eaten at all before school began. Yet all were required to wait until 10:00 A.M. to get a snack. At this point some children were overly hungry and went after the snacks frantically. Other children who were not hungry had to stop their creative play to eat—an unnecessary distraction. And many children, even though they weren't hungry, felt compelled to eat because there wouldn't be any snack later.

When Jeff discussed this situation with us, we suggested that the day care center abandon the snacktime altogether and set up a snack table in a corner of the room where the children could go throughout the day whenever they were hungry. "Too much chaos!" "Too much mess!" "Impossible!" were the initial responses.

After much discussion the staff decided to try our suggestion: They put out plastic pitchers of juice and paper cups in addition to snack foods that the children could handle without assistance. They found that some children who never ate breakfast made a beeline for the snacks as soon as they arrived. Other children didn't stop their morning play to eat a snack. Some of the children who had previously snacked when they weren't really hungry and picked at their lunch now snacked earlier and ate heartily at lunchtime. The center found that this approach cut down dramatically on waste. When they had an appointed snacktime and children were given predetermined amounts of food and drink, the staff would throw away about as much as was eaten. Now those who took a snack ate it because they were genuinely hungry, and the others didn't touch the food at all. There was great comfort for all the children just knowing that snacks were in the room and always available.

After this experience with the snacks, the day care center director said she wished she could figure out a way to apply this method to lunchtime as well. But with so many children, she was afraid things might be too chaotic if children were eating lunches over an extended period of time. We suggested that they set up an eating area and assign a staff member to kitchen duty for a two-hour period each day. Children who bring lunch could get their lunch boxes from the kitchen and eat whenever they were hungry. If the school prepared lunch for the children, the lunches could be kept available (for example, soup, sandwiches, juices and fruits) during the extended lunch period. In the event a child was not hungry at any time during the appointed lunch hours, she could continue to play or nap and always have the snack table to go to when she became hungry. Certain "lunch foods" that don't need to be heated or served could be transferred to the snack table and be made available to children. The center is presently planning to implement this approach.

You may want to suggest this approach to your nursery or day care center or ask the person caring for your child at home to apply it. The idea may be met with surprise or resistance, but persevere. Even if the center will not apply this approach generally, you should urge that your child be allowed to eat the foods he brings with him whenever he is hungry. Baby-sitters can usually accept these instructions if you impress upon them their importance.

LABELS

This is the age when many parents begin to attach labels to their children's eating behavior. "My child is a finicky eater." "Oh, mine is a dawdler; she takes all day with her food." "My Timmy wolfs down his food. We call him the steam shovel." "Deborah is such a picky and fussy eater that we call her Miss Fuss-Pot." "Sasha eats all day long; she's a little piggy."

Labels are very dangerous. Obviously, they damage the self-esteem of the child who in one way or another hears the message. Secondly, though they may describe the child at a particular moment, labels arrest psychological development because the child is slotted into a particular way of being and often behaves as the label suggests—this is what is known as a self-fulfilling prophecy.

The label is rarely accurate and generally reflects the parents' uninformed preconceptions and concerns. The child who is labeled "finicky" may be very selective in her food choices. This is not a bad thing to be when making important decisions about your body's needs and defining your preferences. The child who dawdles, which is typical for this age group, may need more time than another child her age to finish her food. What's the rush? Some children prefer leisurely dining to the quick pace many of us have adopted. Try to adjust yourself and figure out what you can do while she eats slowly. You don't have to keep her company until she finishes, but don't leave as a punishment. Just explain that she can take her time but that you must do some chores while she finishes up. If you need to get out of the house with her, wrap up what she is eating or take with you finger foods you know she likes.

The child who wolfs down his food and eats with gusto and enjoyment shouldn't be praised or criticized either. It's just the way he eats right now. He may be very hungry. He may like the feel of a lot of food in his mouth. He may be eating quickly in order to get back to other things. Try to give him the leeway he needs. Labeling the child or his behavior can have no beneficial effect and can be damaging.

THE EXPANDING WORLD

As your child starts nursery school or day care, watches TV and plays with other children, you may see a shift in her eating patterns: "Lois loved my homemade soups. One day after school she brought home a friend. When I put the soup on the table, her little friend said, 'No, thank you. I hate soup. I never eat it.' Wouldn't you know, Lois refused to eat it as well. Weeks have passed, and she still won't eat my soups."

This is fairly typical behavior. Lois wants her friend's approval and wants to be like her. Imitation is extremely common with children at this age. It has nothing to do with the food. If Lois's friend had said, "Why do you wear dresses to school? I hate dresses and won't wear them," most likely Lois would tell her mom that she wants to wear pants from now on. You may want to remind your child that she can have different tastes from her good friend's. Her tummy is different, and people who like each other a lot don't always eat the same thing. But from our experience this explanation usually doesn't work. You'll have to allow this stage of identification and imitation to play itself out.

Another question is what to do about TV. The ads are very enticing and capture a young child's fancy—especially those sugar-coated cereal ads. Keep the cereals available along with other brands and remember not to make a particular fuss about the cereal requested. You may want to ask your child if she really likes the cereal or if it's the box she is attracted to. One parent caught on to the fact that the child was enticed by the box with E.T. on it and by the shape of the cereal inside. He gave his daughter the box and some of the cereal to play with while she ate her rice cereal. You can explain to your child about food values but don't deny her the cereal of her choice. Keep in mind that if no fuss is made, your child can decide for herself what feels best in her body. Also if your child eats with hunger and stops when full, she will be eating small amounts of the disapproved cereal. No harm will come of it.

You're walking down the street and your three-year-old starts pulling at you. "I want an ice cream, gum from the machine, a doughnut, a hamburger." Children are visually oriented. The advertising and marketing experts know this and capitalize on children's impulses. What should a parent do? The first question should be "Are you hungry?" If she says yes, you might let her choose one thing to buy from the store or a street vendor. We urge parents to carry food when they're on outings with their children. Tell the children that you have what they need with you in case they get hungry. Tell them, before they are bombarded by the smell and sight of food, that the outing is not for food shopping. In other words make it clear before you leave home whether they will be allowed to buy food when they get hungry or whether you're carrying food for them.

MANNERS

Just a short word about manners: We would caution parents of this age group not to make eating a negative experience by excessive pressure about table manners. Of course, parents want to socialize their children, and many parents find their children's eating behavior very offensive. But we urge you to be sensitive to the age-appropriateness of your demands. Your two-, three-, and even four-year-old will spill milk, drop food, dribble, wiggle in her chair and so on. Much of this has to do with her activity level and her motor coordination. When your child is severely chastised for conduct beyond her control developmentally, it hurts her; it doesn't lead to the desired results; and it ruins the eating experience for everybody. This does not mean that you're not allowed to guide your child. When the proper time comes, you can gently begin explaining what is acceptable behavior in your household. "Yes, you can eat cookies, but not throughout the house, only in the kitchen." "Soup is easier to eat with a spoon instead of the fork you are using." "No, boiled peas are different from marbles." "Milk is fun to dribble down the high chair, but if you want to dribble, you can dribble water in the bathtub instead." All this is said in the spirit of recognition and support for her curiosity. At the same time you are informing her what behavior is acceptable to you.

11

THE MIDDLE YEARS:
FIVE THROUGH TEN

The great developmental growth that occurs during the middle years, from five through ten, will bring with it great changes in eating behavior. At five your child may ask you to help him cut food, pour, butter corn, and so on. By ten, he completely feeds himself and has probably added shopping and cooking to his repertoire. Between the ages of five and ten the variety of foods eaten steadily expands, and your ten-year-old generally has a full range of foods on his menu.

During these middle years the peer group takes on great importance. A child may have one or a series of "best" friends, group activities are common and the "gang" takes precedence. The ups and downs of these relationships are brought home, and parents must deal with group norms as they are quoted by the children: "Randi stays up until nine o'clock, why can't I?" "Josh's parents let him eat dinner watching TV, why can't we?"

During this period the child moves from a certain amount of dependence to the point where, in many situations, she no longer needs you. Parents can have a very difficult time in these middle years trying to calculate exactly when it is appropriate to grant freedom and when to set limits and controls.

When do we let our children cross the street alone, go to the store alone, select their daytime activities, decide their bedtime? We can be sure the child in these years will seek to test the limits that you set and to challenge you.

If the self-demand feeding approach is followed, this is one area where there should be minimal contention. The child has the freedom to choose when, what and how much he will eat at all times. He may develop his own peculiarities in this respect, but it is critical that his eating decisions not be interfered with. He is fully capable of regulating his own food intake. Allowing him to do so can be a source of pleasure for you both.

Because of the individuality of each child and because of the uneven path of growth, it's hard to predict the precise age at which various eating issues will arise in these middle years. However, these pages will highlight some of the common situations and show how the self-demand feeding approach can help.

If you have not yet been using self-demand feeding, then hunger is the first issue to tackle. The phrase "Are you hungry?" must become as familiar as "Good morning" until your child clearly equates eating with physical hunger. At five, a child is perfectly able to tell you when she is hungry. Hunger may occur several times during the day. She may prefer snacking to meals or prefer one meal to others. She may not always want to eat with the family.

Because the child is at school part of the day, where parents can't monitor eating, the "good breakfast" often becomes a big issue in the house. Many children are not hungry for breakfast. Like certain adults, they simply don't wake up hungry or experience hunger as they busily prepare to go off to school. Don't force your child to eat an unwanted breakfast. It's a hopeless struggle that starts the day off wrong. Instead prepare snacks for her to carry in her pockets or lunch box so that she can feed herself when she feels hungry. If your child *does* want breakfast and is also a slow starter in the morning, it is a good idea to get her up a half hour early so that she can eat and be ready for school on time. You may want to announce to her how much time she has until she must leave and what's available to eat. Then leave it up to her. If she is really hungry, she will adjust her schedule, especially after missing a few breakfasts because of her tardiness. But don't panic if she continues to miss breakfast. She will satisfy her hunger by eating the snacks she carries with her. These and the other foods she eats during the day will provide more than ample nutrition.

Some foods are easier to eat than others, and you can save yourself a lot of trouble if you figure out which easy foods your child likes. These may include sandwiches, cheese or jam on crackers, eggs, fruit, yogurt, puddings, pretzels, carrot or other vegetable sticks, cookies. It is a blessing that children this age appreciate and want such foods, since they are just as nutritious as cooked meals, can be served in a few minutes and rarely involve much cleaning up. This frees you to cook for yourself what *you* would like to eat without having to worry about cooking several items at once. Allow your children their easy foods until their tastes become more complicated.

As your child's preferences broaden, it is important to have a full stock of these foods available. To keep tabs on her current tastes, get her to participate in preparing the weekly shopping list. Even your five-year-old will tell you her likes and dislikes, and buying the foods she prefers will mean minimal waste and struggle.

In the middle years children become quite discriminating about what they will eat. Foods may be refused for a variety of reasons—color, texture, smell, taste. Six-year-old Marion won't eat the crust of the bread because "it is too hard." Seven-year-old Stan won't eat watermelon because "it's too wet." Another child won't eat her meat unless all the fat is trimmed off. Eight-year-old John thinks eggs are "too slimy to eat." Nine-year-old Jenny says she won't eat Jell-o because "Jell-o shakes too much." These are normal responses. It is futile to argue with children about their tastes.

Certain food rituals may appear. Nine-year-old Joan ate her foods in a very particular order, one at a time: first the potato, pasta or rice, then the vegetable and finally the meat. Richard, her brother, adopted a dramatically opposite ritual. Given a good base like mashed potatoes, Richard mushed in the peas and cut up the meat to create his own version of shepherd's pie. In fact, if the concoction had the proper consistency, it was invariably sculptured into a shape to Richard's liking. Fortunately, Joan and Richard's parents saw no reason to create an issue about their children's idiosyncratic styles. The children were happy, and these peculiar little food games did not interfere with their eating.

The most common breach of custom with this approach is the meal that starts with dessert. Don't fight it. Children raised on self-demand feeding have often begun with ice cream and moved on to the vegetable or meat. Frequently when the child is hungry, he has a particular food in mind to fill that hunger. So even if he eats only ice cream during a meal, let him have it. If his body needed something else, he would be the first to know and would ask for it. Trust his ability to be in charge of his own eating. As we've discussed, if he's new to the self-demand feeding approach, there will be an inordinate interest in the previously forbidden foods. The demand for ice cream when you are starting dinner may be to test *you*. DON'T FLUNK THE TEST! For this approach to work it is essential that the child be absolutely clear that he is making the decisions about when, what and how much he will eat.

Children in the middle years will also go on food jags, often with newfound favorites. When six-year-old Carl tasted pizza for the first time, he loved it and wanted to eat it at every meal for days at a time. It was a new discovery that captured both his imagination and his taste buds. Allow these fads to run their course. It is equally common for the youngster's tastes to change and the previous favorite—pizza—to be entirely abandoned.

Dinner

Many parents attempting self-demand feeding are most disturbed by the threatened loss of the family dinner hour. The concept of a dinner hour, however, assumes that there is a specific time in the evening when everyone in the household is hungry and wants to eat—*and* has an appetite for exactly the same foods. Obviously, if children are on self-demand feeding, their hunger will not always coincide with the rest of the family's. If sitting down to dinner is important to you, preserve this ritual for yourself but don't push a child to eat when he's not hungry. If "dinner" in your family means time for you to socialize with your children, invite them to join you in talk without necessarily eating.

Your child may find it difficult to sit still through a family meal. She may want to sit on her knees, rock in her chair, talk a lot, fiddle with food or utensils. Eating is interrupted by all this activity and sometimes by dawdling. This may not be your idea of proper mealtime behavior. You have come home from a day of work, and prepared foods you like and you want a leisurely and relaxing dinner. Your child cannot understand this kind of pacing. Before you ask her to join you at the evening meal, ask her if she is hungry. If the answer is no, you might invite her to sit with you for a while and tell you about her day. She should be permitted to leave the table and resume a different activity when her attention span wanders. Your approach should be the same when she comes to the table hungry: When she has satisfied her appetite, pe mit her to leave.

If your child comes to the table but is not hungry for any of the foods being served, allow her to pick a food that is readily available and needs little or no preparation. Obviously, you will not prepare another meal. Most children in this age range can be quite easily satisfied with substitutes when a supply of foods they like is available.

More and more during these elementary school years your child establishes a personal agenda. He has his own idea of what he wants to do, of the interests he wants to pursue, of the friends he wants to be with. Eating or mealtimes can be an interruption of his agenda. He may not want to leave his friends to come home for dinner. He may not want to put down the book he is reading or to tear himself away from a TV show. He may want to perform the magic show he has been practicing all afternoon or continue playing with his dolls or board games. Sometimes, he will want to bring these activities to the table. He may bolt down the food to get back to his play or he may ignore hunger signals so that he can stay with the current activity. If you are like most parents, you will worry and feel he needs your help. Don't force him to conform. Remind him to take time out to eat and inquire whether he is hungry. But remember about self-regulation. It's great that he can become so involved in his activity. Don't worry; he will eat when he gets hungry enough.

You might ask, "Does this mean that when we parents finish our dinner, we have to cook again for each child as she demands food?" Of course you don't. Here are some other options:

116

- Leave a portion of dinner warming on the stove or in the oven. When your child gets hungry, she can help herself.
- The child can help herself to foods in the refrigerator or foods on her food shelf that need no preparation.
- Older children can prepare or cook simple dishes for themselves.

There is no need for chaos or for you to be enslaved in the kitchen. The joy of children of this age is their ability to do for themselves. Just be sure to tell them what's available. They can help themselves when they get hungry.

These are also the years when the child's friends begin to stay for dinner and when he will want to eat at his friends' homes. Here's a situation that arose under these circumstances: Peter invited Josh for dinner and said, "At my house you can have whatever you want to eat when you are hungry." Nine-year-old Josh didn't believe him. When, at six, Peter's mother, Miriam, asked them if they were hungry, Josh said he was hungry but would love ice cream instead of the prepared meal. Miriam gave him the ice cream. Later that evening, Miriam got a phone call from Sally, Josh's mother. The conversation went something like this:

SALLY: Hello, Miriam. Josh had a wonderful time playing with Peter. Thank you for having him over. He told me some tall story that you gave him ice cream for dinner. That's not true, is it?

MIRIAM: Yes, it is true.

SALLY: How is that possible?

(Miriam explained to Sally how self-demand feeding works and her confidence in the method. Sally was shocked.)

SALLY: This is hard to believe. Let me tell you, we don't allow many sweets in our house, and you can't have a treat like ice cream without eating a proper meal first. This dinner is going to cause us real problems.

MIRIAM: Look, I'm sorry. Next time Josh comes over, I can explain to him what we're doing, but it would be hard for me to force him to eat a meal when I don't do that with Peter.

SALLY: Well, what do you think will happen when Peter comes to eat at our house and tells me he'd like pea-

117

nut butter and jelly sandwiches when I call the boys to dinner?

MIRIAM: I hope you let him have it. But if that's hard for you, I guess the best thing is to ask him to choose something from what you've got, if he's hungry. That will take the edge off his hunger, and then when he gets home, he can have the peanut butter and jelly.

SALLY: Well, I can't let him have whatever he wants without doing the same for my children and I'm certainly not prepared to do that.

MIRIAM: Look, Sally, you don't have to change because of us. We'll just explain to Peter that you do things differently. I don't think he'll care at all. He's probably much more interested in being with Josh than in what he's going to eat.

Dining Out

A parent in one of our workshops said that she looked forward to her child's reaching five or six as a time when she could begin eating at restaurants with the family. She found to her dismay that six-year-old Penny was rarely interested in the restaurant food and became restless and uncontrollable during these meals.

Restaurant eating is often problematic at this age. For one thing, it may be very difficult to arrange to go out when the child is hungry. The restaurants that most adults like may not carry fare that is appealing to children. Asking the active child to sit quietly in a restaurant may be demanding more than she is capable of.

Going into this situation is often destined to be unpleasant. It's best not to take children to restaurants where you can't get the foods they want and where the child's age-appropriate behavior will be out of place. If you're traveling, or for other reasons find it necessary to go out to eat, bring the child's foods along if the restaurant doesn't have them. Also bring with you table toys, such as books, crayons, paper, Legos and so on so that the youngster can play while you enjoy your meal.

Some children, naturally, will love to eat out. They look forward to selecting food from the menu, talking to the waiter, looking at others in the restaurant and generally love the sense of being grown up enough to go out with their parents. They may even associate certain favorite dishes with a particular restaurant and save their appetite for that event.

Manners

This is not a book on manners, etiquette or how you should discipline or socialize your child. However, these questions do arise at the dining table. In fact, for many families, mealtime has been the main stage for the struggle around socialization. The self-demand feeding approach will eliminate the struggle over when, what and how much is eaten, but the question of eating behavior and table manners will still need to be dealt with. In the interest of providing a calm and pleasant eating experience, parents have to weigh the necessity of placing constraints on their child's eating behavior. Children and adults have different views, experiences, mental and motor capacities, values and interests. Children see the world from a different perspective than adults. You may think it is important that the tuna fish salad not be eaten with fingers. Your six-year-old thinks it is most important that the tuna fish gets to his mouth in the easiest and quickest way—with his fingers. We can influence and control our children's conduct, but if we are sensitive and reasonable in setting limits, we will find ways to allow the child to assert his independence as a decision-making person.

Consider carefully whether the eating rules you are setting are age-appropriate. For example, if your five-year-old is still struggling with a knife, cut his food for him or let him use his fingers. You can encourage him to use the utensils but don't press the issue to the point where it interferes with his eating. (At fourteen, on the other hand, he would be in big trouble if he's still asking you to cut his meat!) If your six-year-old always chews with her mouth open, it may be because she is not yet of an age to control this behavior or it may be uncomfortable for her to do so. The way she chews is natural for her at the moment. An attempt to alter this behavior will only spoil her eating experience. It is not worth it. However, if she's throwing her green peas at her brother, tell her to stop and ask her if she wants to leave the table.

We also encourage parents to question if the eating customs

that they were brought up with and would impose on their children make sense. In our view, many of these customs are arbitrary and could be profitably abandoned. For example, one mother told this story: "My mother taught me that you shouldn't eat while standing. I attempted to impose this on my five-year-old, who questioned the rationale for this rule. I really didn't have one. As time went on, there were other rules that I could not justify, and I finally gave them up. Now my children may put their elbows on the table and be comfortable; they don't try to suppress a burp; they can start eating before everyone else is served, while their food is still hot; they are permitted to talk with food in their mouth. Now that these rules have been lifted, I have found there are fewer struggles at the dinner table."

This mother took her children's questions about adult manners seriously. She realized that some of the rules she had considered essential to dinner table behavior really made no sense from her children's point of view. She decided that she could live with elbows on the table and could better explain to them when they were older and had more control that some things, such as chewing with their mouth open, were not generally acceptable in the world. The fact of the matter is that if you, the parent, observe certain decorum, your children will, more than likely, eventually imitate you. As they get older, they will be anxious to "do things right" socially, and that will be the time that the finer points of table manners will be better accepted.

Parents' Food Values

Just as your child increasingly wants to determine his own agenda, he is also developing a reasoning and questioning mind. Your elementary school child can challenge your requests, demands and opinions. You can tell your child what you want him to have in his diet, and he will ask you why. These are the years when you may want to impress on your child your own food values. This can create struggles.

You explain to your nine-year-old that some foods are junk, you are opposed to his eating them and, furthermore, you feel that the production and distribution of such products represent all that is plastic and unnatural in America. Your child may not accept this explanation with the calm and composure you would like. He may throw up arguments: "If it's so bad, why are so many other kids allowed to eat junk?" or "I like things that are plastic," or "On TV they say these foods taste good, give you energy and make you strong." As we have said throughout this book, the less fuss you make about your child's food choices, the less likely it will be that the food arena becomes the stage on which the struggle for independence is played out. In fact, when the controls are minimal or nonexistent, children tend to eat pretty much what their parents eat.

The Misuse of Food

Although many of your child's challenges may be genuine, some may be a way of getting your attention. We know that if children don't get positive attention, they will set up situations to get negative attention, rather than settle for no attention at all. Iris is a ten-year-old and the eldest of four daughters. She has always been the little mother in the house. She does extremely well at school and basically is the "good child," the one everyone can depend upon. Her only problem is her eating. Her mother is constantly monitoring her food intake because, "she cannot exercise control for herself." As a consequence, Iris has gained a lot of weight. When we started to work with her, it became apparent that she did not want to give up this problem too quickly because it was one of the very few ways, negative though it was, that she and her mother interacted. Her mother had her hands full with four children and a full-time job. Iris could always be sure to get the attention she craved if it centered around her eating problem.

When this was pointed out, mother and daughter began to work out a relationship independent of Iris's eating. Her mother set aside special time to spend with Iris each evening after the younger children went to sleep. They used the time to talk and to work on a puppet-making project that interested Iris a great deal. Her mother taught her how to use papier-mâché for the head of the puppet, how to select materials and threads for making costumes, and how to sew on her sewing machine. In this relationship Iris was treated like a growing child, not like a little mother. Iris's mother was also urged to stop monitoring Iris's food intake and to avoid criticizing her eating behavior or her weight. As Iris got positive attention directly, the eating problem began to lose its value.

Even children on self-demand feeding may, from time to time, create eating issues to gain attention. If you notice that your child is constantly engaging you in food struggles or eating in a way that seems calculated to draw a response, you should address the situation head on by asking if there is something else he wants. Would he like to have a conversation with you? Does he want to tell you what happened that day? Would he like to play a game, go for a walk, have a moment of cuddling? Is there something upsetting him that he needs to talk about? Again, your aim is to avoid having food become the medium through which other problems are expressed.

When there is more than one adult raising a child, there may be conflicts about food and eating patterns in the household, just as there are with other aspects of child rearing. Children often pick up on disagreements and use them to get the adults' attention, to challenge one of the adults, to pit adults against each other or to please an adult. Robbie, age nine, begins to drench his scrambled eggs in ketchup. Mom looks on with disgust written all over her face. Robbie turns to her and says, "Why the look, Mom? Daddy uses ketchup all the time." Robbie knows that his mother thinks ketchup is "bad" because of its sugar and salt content and that his dad rarely eats any food without it. He has chosen to provoke his mother by ostentatiously adopting his father's habit. His behavior has nothing to do with physical hunger and little to do with personal taste. Keep an eye out for this kind of misuse of food. See if you can let your child make his own choice based on his hunger, even though the adults are skirmishing.

Probably Robbie's mother would have done best not to make a face and to avoid commenting on Robbie's use of the ketchup. All of us know how difficult this sort of restraint is. If Robbie's mother absolutely had to comment, it would have been enough to say, "Robbie, you do not have to do exactly what Dad does with his food. If you really like ketchup, okay, but I hope you can find out for yourself what tastes good to you." This lets Robbie know that you understand why he is using the ketchup and that he'll be happiest if he eats in concert with his own tastes and not for ulterior motives.

During these middle years, eating for emotional reasons can

become a pattern that is hard to break. Children may turn to food when they are bored and in need of distraction, or to relieve anxiety and soothe themselves, or if they are lonely, or in response to changes in the family situation.

When Paula was eleven years old, her mother went to work for the first time. In addition to coming home to an empty house, Paula's new responsibilities involved shopping for and starting dinner and setting the table. Paula felt both burdened and lonely. Very bright and verbal, she missed having someone to talk to when she came home. Paula began overeating. She would nibble on foods as she was doing her chores, using food to pass the time and make her feel less lonely.

Paula's mother understood that this misuse of food was really a sign of the disruption in her daughter's life. Every afternoon on her break from work, she would call home. This gave the child some contact with her mother and a time to talk about her day. Together they planned activities for Paula to do alone and with her friends in the afternoon. The afternoon began to feel less like an empty stretch of time with only chores to do. With time, Paula became more comfortable with the change in her family situation and she turned to food less often to fill the gap.

Martha, the mother of eight-year-old Janice, noticed a change in her daughter's eating pattern. Janice had been using the self-demand feeding approach for several years and had been having a snack after school and then going out to play with her friends. When she got home, she would play independently before dinner. Now, she began eating immediately after being with her friends, and when asked if she was hungry, Janice would say, "I guess so." When Martha asked her daughter if something was bothering her, she was met with a shrug. For two weeks Martha continued to ask Janice gently what was wrong, though she did not make a fuss about her eating. Finally, Janice came home from school in tears and blurted out that she couldn't stand it anymore. Her best friend, Annie, was getting really friendly with another classmate, and Janice was being excluded from activities and secrets.

Martha's sensitivity and her awareness that food was probably not the issue allowed the real problem to surface. If a fuss had been made over the food, this parent could have missed the real issue—Janice's unhappiness about her friend.

Whenever a child's eating behavior becomes the central

focus, there is a real risk that the problem that led to the eating will be totally masked. The child herself may lose sight of what issue caused her unhappy feeling. In Janice's case, it might have looked something like this: Janice's mother noting Janice's increased eating begins to question or criticize this conduct. Perhaps she also notices and expresses the view that Janice is putting on some weight. Janice begins to feel bad *about both the eating and her weight.* She begins to think negatively about herself. She says to herself, "I eat too much; I'm too fat." This self-criticism may cause Janice to lose sight of the original source of her unhappiness—the problem of being excluded from play by her friends. She may even explain her unhappiness in terms of the food and weight: "The reason no one likes me is because I'm too fat." The result of all this is that she doesn't deal with the underlying problem directly. Instead a new problem has been created in its place. As long as the focus remains on the eating, little progress is likely. If you believe that your child is turning to food for psychological reasons, try to stay clear of an involvement with the eating issues and allow space for the real issues to emerge so they can be dealt with.

A poignant incident occurred in a four-week workshop. Lois, the mother of a six-year-old, was completely stymied by an ongoing feeding problem. Sheila dawdled over her food at home and at school. Recurrent dialogues at the table went like this:

SHEILA: I don't want any more.
MOTHER: You haven't eaten more than two bites in half an hour. At least finish your hamburger.
SHEILA: Okay, two more bites.
MOTHER: Five more bites.
SHEILA: Okay, three more bites.
MOTHER: Sheila, why does it take you one hour to eat supper? Just talk less and concentrate on eating. The rest of us finished half an hour ago.
SHEILA: I don't know. I'm eating.
MOTHER: Okay, that's enough. Just get up.
SHEILA: But I'm still very hungry.
MOTHER: Okay, five more minutes.

After several weeks of consultation with us, Lois was able to talk about the illness and death, two years before, of a sibling four years older than Sheila. The illness had required that Lois feed her older daughter, and the feedings took a long time, with periods of rest between bites of food. Sheila, who had been very attached to her sister, was a witness to all of this. As this tragic situation was discussed, it seemed possible that Sheila was dawdling over her food as a way of holding on to the memory of her sister; she was trying to get the loving care that she saw her mother give to her sick sister.

Understandably, Sheila's parents wanted to protect both their daughter and themselves from these sad memories, but what was not being talked about was being acted out behaviorally in the feeding situation. We felt that her sister's death had to be discussed. When Sheila was dawdling over her food, she could be asked if she was thinking about her sister and remembering how long it took her to eat and how much time her mother had had to spend feeding and taking care of her. Sheila could then talk about her sadness and feelings of loss. We instructed Sheila's mother to say, "I remember how much time it took for me to feed your sister. It must have been hard for you at those times." Sheila needs room to express not only her sad feelings but also her angry ones. This will help her say in words what she's saying in her eating behavior.

Parental Baggage

During these middle years, we may closely identify with our children and want to save them from the pain and heartaches we may have endured at their age because of a weight problem.

Anna, mother of ten-year-old Josh, was overweight when she was young and remembered these years as "torture." She became intensely preoccupied with Josh's eating and weight as he approached adolescence, and his appetite increased. "I don't ever want my child to go through what I went through," she said, and began hounding her son about his eating. "Don't eat the bread." "No, we are not going to have spaghetti again this week; it's too fattening." "Why don't you have a piece of fruit for dessert instead of that cookie?" She would watch Josh for any increase in weight, and though he was not completely comfortable with his weight gain, his mother's preoccupation made him angry. The more she hounded him, the more he ate. Soon he was eating to get back at her and to stuff down his anger. This is a common occurrence: Children as well as adults who have difficulty expressing anger frequently turn to food.

Anna did not understand that her son's increased appetite was probably temporary and that his eating pattern would not necessarily mirror her own lifelong struggle with food. Ironically, by focusing on the food issue, Anna was exacerbating the very situation she had hoped to prevent. If children are eating on demand and food and weight issues are not permitted to escalate into major concerns, the great likelihood is that the underlying problems will be revealed and dealt with and that a normal and comfortable body weight will be attained. Overreacting when a child's eating patterns change or when he gains weight gets in the way of this process.

12

THE TURBULENT TEENS

The last stage of childhood, the preteen and teenage years, is often accompanied by growing pains for parents as well as for children. This is the phase when children must finally work through the issue of separation from home. It can be a time of great ambivalence. One day you see a budding adult, the next day a babbling child. Your fourteen-year-old is demanding freedom of choice to do what he pleases and to come and go as he wants: "All the other kids can stay out till midnight, why can't I?" "I'm going to meet my friends when I finish my homework." Yet, this same teenager has the insecurities of a younger child, "I don't want to take the bus home, I want you to pick me up." "I don't want you to go out tonight; the house seems creepy without you." These contradictions are a normal part of teenage development and often extend to all areas of activity.

Characteristic of adolescence is "hanging out" with friends at hamburger joints, pizza parlors, street corners, bowling alleys, baseball fields, parks, the local shopping center and other friends' houses. What she does at these places, what she talks and thinks about is often considered "none of your business." She demands privacy—"Just leave me alone." Though you used to hear lengthy accounts of the day's events, you are now confronted with monosyllabic answers to most questions. At one time she looked to you for advice, comfort and structure, but now she turns to others, usually the peer group, for information, support and activity. The process of identity formation and separation from you, the parents, is in full swing.

Differences in gender roles are taking a more adult shape. Teenage boys often begin working hard at achieving the appearance of manhood. They may adopt macho poses, wanting to appear tough, independent and athletic. At the same time they may not have outgrown many of their fears, though they hide them lest they be considered "sissy."

Girls are developing breasts, beginning menstruation and preparing for womanhood. Being attractive becomes terribly important and there is a focus, often a preoccupation, on clothing, makeup and hair-styles. Most teenage girls measure themselves by physical attributes and development: They think that who they are is closely connected with how they look. Even for girls who want to achieve academically and athletically, it is difficult not to feel pressured by the society's emphasis on appearance.

Teenagers are immensely involved with their bodies. For girls the desire is to be thin; for boys, to be strong and muscular. Standing in front of the mirror, sucking in tummies, flexing muscles, taking stock from the front, side and back, looking for hair growth and pimples, are major activities for the teenager. Adolescents can be extremely critical of their bodies from head to toe. "My hair is too curly (straight)." "My nose is too big (small)." "My shoulders are too broad (narrow)." "My legs are too fat (skinny)." "My toes are too long (short)." Teenagers are busy comparing themselves with their friends and the latest idols; they try to change what they don't like.

One mother spoke of spending her teenage years trying to get rid of her freckles, which, until she was thirteen, had been considered "cute." She tried various remedies, from lemon juice to peroxide to almond extract, to get rid of them. Her mother's explanations about pigmentation and how the freckles would probably fade with time were met with cries of disbelief and sorrow. Now she understands very well her teenage daughter's preoccupation with straightening her frizzy hair.

Body awareness begins much earlier for any child, but in adolescence interest in body size is intense. If your child has been using the self-demand feeding approach, you need only allow her to continue on this path. Her freedom to make her own decisions about food should remain unimpaired. Body changes, which certainly will occur, should not be a signal to impose controls. However, you may need to help your teenager deal with the cultural predilection for imposing eating rules. Reading this chapter *with* your teen can help both of you target the areas where potential difficulties may arise.

If you are a parent of a teenager who has never been exposed to the self-demand feeding concept, we suggest the following:

- Buy your child his own copy of this book so that he can read it, mark it and refer back to it at his own pace. Fix a time each week when you and your teenager will meet to discuss separate chapters. We suggest he start with chapters two, three, four and six before reading this and the following chapters.
- Use each section to begin to set up ways to implement this approach.
- Begin by having a range of foods available that your teenager likes.
- Allow your child to determine when, what and how much he wants to eat (chapter four).
- Focus on physical hunger as the reason for eating (chapter three).
- Be prepared to deal with your own biases about how teenagers "should" eat.
- Do not impose your rules about food and eating on your child.
- Allow for much testing by your teenager.
- Remember that your teenager is developing his own tastes and eating style. If there is not too much parental meddling, his eating decisions will reflect his physiological needs and not his resistance to parental control.

"Ma, What Is There to Eat?"

This may be a familiar cry as your ravenous teenager bolts into the house from his day's activities. One mother's experience: "One of the toughest jobs I've had lately with my fifteen-year-old, Chuck, has been trying to keep him full from four P.M., when he gets home from school, until he goes to bed. He is always hungry, and I spend my life stocking the refrigerator and kitchen shelves. When he brings friends home with him, I sometimes feel there will never be enough food and drink to go around. What happened to that wonderful, moderate appetite he used to have?"

Many parents talk about being "eaten out of house and home" when their children hit adolescence. Your teenager has no interest in keeping you permanently at the supermarket checkout line. Rather, she is eating a lot because she is growing. Most teenagers use up enormous amounts of energy. Their days are longer. They may be getting into athletics in a serious way. They are running around with friends. They go to parties and dance for hours at a stretch. New energy is sparked by sexual interest, politics and community activities. Arguing and negotiating with you as they try to come into their own also burns up calories!

As we have said, you will never see as much physical growth and weight gain as in the first year of life, but adolescence is a close second. During these years the body attains adult proportions. Adolescents may grow three to four inches a year, and their weight almost doubles between the onset of puberty and age eighteen.

If your teenager is eating enormous quantities in response to physical appetite, let him eat. Efforts to put the brakes on are doomed. The consequences of saying "That's enough!" are almost always upsetting. One teen explained, "My parents constantly tell me I eat too much. I feel insulted and I hate their telling me what to do." He felt he was being controlled at a time when he was trying to establish his own control and make his own decisions.

Of course, during their child's teenage years, parents often find themselves facing new situations where limits must be set. Cigarette smoking, drugs, sex, drinking and many other areas of behavior may require parental supervision and even strict rules. Knowing when and where to draw the line and when to trust your child is the major task of these years. But the child's eating decisions should remain her own, a zone of noninterference.

What can you do when it feels as if you're always cooking and shopping for a seemingly insatiable child? Why not avoid the problem by having your child pitch in? Your teenager can certainly do the supermarket shopping. And perhaps there could be a cooking jamboree one evening or weekend day—with the whole family participating—so that there will be food available for the coming week. You might consider giving your teenager a food allowance so that he can purchase his own foods, freeing you of some of this responsibility.

Another issue parents frequently find baffling is how to satisfy the varied palates of their teenagers. A shopping list should reflect the food desires of all family members. In one family where there are two teenage boys and a younger child, they have called this the "cravings" list. Their mother attaches it to the refrigerator, and the boys write on it each week. When the self-demand feeding approach was first introduced in this home, the list included all the foods that had been denied or were considered special. Prominent were soda, sugar-coated cereal and candy bars. The seven-year-old, when first faced with the choice, put Tide detergent on his cravings list. Though that became a family joke, it demonstrated the difficulty some children may have in freeing themselves from their parents' judgments. This boy wanted to please his mother and did not really trust that his food "craving" would be met with approval.

The food lists of teenagers may reflect new life-style interests. One mother spoke about her son who recently declared he was a vegetarian. He did not really like vegetables, but with his newfound concern for the plight of animals, his diet changed. A father explained his surprise when his son declared he wanted to "keep kosher." This father had struggled to separate from his own orthodox Jewish upbringing and now was faced with his son's desire to pursue what he had moved away from. One mother spoke about her daughter's "macrobiotic" diet and her concern about whether this was a healthy program for a still-growing child. Her daughter had become interested in Eastern religion and philosophy and insisted on eating only brown rice, steamed and raw vegetables and so on.

When your teenager embarks on a new food regime, she is trying to define herself and needs the space to do this without excessive interference. Such interference sets the stage for food preferences to become the locus of struggle, while the real issue, the attempt at self-definition, gets buried. Although you may be concerned about the nutritional safety of some of these eating philosophies, we've found that, in almost every instance, the child ends up regulating herself after she's had a chance to see how she feels on the special diet.

Fran, the mother of three teenage daughters, told us how she managed to feed her family and not go crazy. "I decided long before I ever heard about self-demand feeding that children know best what they want to eat and that there's no use pushing them. When my kids were in high school, I was struck by the fact that they had very different eating habits. One was a strict vegetarian, the other only liked a few foods, peanut butter being her favorite, and the youngest would eat almost anything. My husband and I both worked full-time. I decided that I would cook one meal a day. Whoever was hungry would eat at that time. This, by the way, turned out to be everyone. Each child could usually find at least one item she liked from what was served. Generally the vegetarian would eat some bread and a vegetable, the one who liked few foods would make herself a peanut butter and jelly sandwich, and the youngest child would eat what my husband or I ate."

Snacking Out

Many teenagers eat on their own schedules; snacking at fast-food joints is their way of life. Parents worry about the nutritional benefits their children get at these places, especially when a steady diet of pizza and soda seems completely acceptable to the teenager.

Trying to interfere raises such family tensions that it is important for parents to evaluate their conception of "junk" food. Fast foods may not be as devoid of nutrients as one might expect. We are not advocates of fast-food eateries, but hamburgers do contain a large amount of protein. Pizza has been described as, "the ideal McGovern food, since it supplies the basic nutrients in approximately the amounts recommended in the Dietary Goals established by Senator George McGovern's nutrition subcommittee. A typical slice of pizza has 15 percent protein, 27 percent fat, and 58 percent carbohydrate. Thus, either as a snack or as part of a meal, it's a reasonably well-balanced food" (Jane Brody, *Jane Brody's Nutrition Book*, p. 396).

Most fast-food diets, of course, are high in fat and sodium and lack fruits, vegetables and fiber. If your teenager is frequenting fast-food places, it is especially important that there be variety of a different sort at home. This will guarantee your child the freedom to choose from other food groups when his body is signaling for a change. In all likelihood he will choose foods that provide what he needs in addition to the hamburger and the soda. When a full range of foods are available, teenagers on self-demand feeding still regulate their diets on their own.

"Ma, I Don't Want to Eat Now!"

A father exclaimed, "I just can't adjust to the change. Barry, my sixteen-year-old son, always ate with us. I looked forward to these dinnertimes together. We never had a rigid, set hour to eat, but it was a time on the weekdays, especially, when I could be with my family and catch up on the day's activities. I really enjoyed these times. Now Barry refuses to eat with us."

Your adolescent may be hungry, but he may not want to eat with the family. He may take his plate, leave the dining table, settle himself in front of the TV and proceed to eat there. Teenagers want to control when they are with their family. You may experience the "empty-chair syndrome."

We interviewed Shirley, the mother of fourteen-year-old Kenny. She told us, "Things are very different since Kenny became a teenager. First of all the foods I cook that he has always loved he no longer will even taste. He is called for dinner and always says, 'I'll be right there,' but never shows up. He prefers taking a plate of food to his room or better yet riding his bike down to the neighborhood fast-food hangout and eating a hot dog, French fries and a Coke. It makes me so angry. Also I don't think that he eats enough. He gets headaches, and I'm sure it's from not eating properly."

We decided to interview Kenny and find out what his side of the story was. He told us, "It's not true that I don't like my mother's cooking. I know she thinks that. Let me just tell you how the conversation goes everyday:

"MOM: It's dinnertime. Are you hungry?
"KEN: Yeah.
"MOM: What do you want to eat?
"KEN: What is there to eat?
"MOM: Just tell me what you want.
"KEN: I don't know.

"Then I get called for dinner. When I go downstairs, my mother has usually cooked something she and my dad like. Many times she knows I don't particularly care for it and then she is surprised and hurt that I don't eat it or that I don't even want to come to the table."

Does this sound like a typical teenage-parent exchange? There certainly is a lack of communication and frustration on both sides. We suggested to Kenny that it is unfair to be angry at his mother for preparing food he dislikes when he is so unclear and nonspecific when she asks him what he wants. If he is hungry, it really is up to him to "read his hunger" and to be very specific as to what particular food will satisfy that hunger cue. We also told Shirley that she should tell Kenny to let her know what foods he wants in the house.

A few days later Shirley reported that Kenny was being very specific about his food requests. He told her, as she was preparing the family dinner, that he wanted spaghetti with butter and cheese. She made it and had it ready but he did not join the others at dinner. When they had finished, Shirley told Kenny to reheat the spaghetti and that his parents were going out to the movies. She then instructed him to do the dishes when he was finished, since he was the last to eat.

Though there's nothing wrong with having a child do the dishes, this time it seemed like a punishment. Shirley needed to work out her feelings about Kenny's solitary eating so that she wouldn't react angrily. She had to see his eating behavior as an expression of his need to move away from his mother, for which he should not be punished.

After a few months both Kenny and Shirley reported much less tension around food. The headaches diminished as well, probably because they had more to do with Kenny's conflicts and tension about separation than with having an empty stomach.

It is understandable that, as parents, we feel a loss of a sense of family at mealtimes. But breaking away from the traditional family mealtime may be part of the general adolescent breaking away. The teenager wants her own agenda. It is a period we have to live through, as our parents probably lived through our adolescent rebellion.

Of course, not all teenagers dislike eating with their families. Many feel that it is the one peaceful time of the day, a ritual that brings the family together, at least for a little while. When no one is forcing the get-together *or* what is eaten, dinner can be an enjoyable time.

Yet, the concept of fixed mealtimes must be called into question. Why do we have a dinnertime? For contact and communication with the family. But does it have to be over food? Does everyone have to eat when the family comes together? It is possible that a fixed dinnertime or mealtime may, in some families, go by the wayside when self-demand feeding is introduced. This happens because the first goal is to get in touch with physical hunger and feed it promptly, which might not occur at "mealtimes." As we described in chapter three, you might consider the possibility of encouraging a gathering time that does not require eating, or else you might allow the children to join you at *your* mealtime without pushing them to eat.

One mother spoke of feeling "so liberated" when her teenagers did not want to eat meals with her. She was freer to invite friends over, to be with her partner, and, at times, to be alone and enjoy a quiet meal without having to interact with anyone. She also discovered that her children did not become malnourished or lethargic about feeding themselves.

Sometimes, parents find their teenagers' behavior at the table unacceptable and rude. This situation is often eased by a willingness to let go of mealtime rules and routine patterns of the past. One mother handled a difficult situation in the following way: "My sixteen-year-old, Alice, and my fourteen-year-old, Lee, were so impossible at mealtimes that I dreaded dinner. They would sit at the table slumped over their plates, and constantly tease and argue with each other. Alice said she didn't like to eat with Lee, and Lee wanted to eat in front of the TV. I realized some solution had to be found, and so I agreed. As a result, Alice was more relaxed at the table without her brother constantly teasing her, Lee enjoyed his meal with TV and I felt much less exhausted at the end of the meal. I hope we can all eat together again, but for right now, this feels fine."

"Ma, I'm Going on a Diet, I'm Getting Too Fat!"

Our nation has an obsession with weight, food and slimness, and the preoccupation is starting with younger and younger children. Look at the ads: Eight-year-olds are displayed wearing skin-tight designer jeans and standing in provocative poses. Young children who see these ads begin to compare themselves to the models and question whether they measure up. By the time they are teenagers, preoccupation with this ideal creates grave problems because it interferes with adolescents finding a weight that is both physiologically and emotionally comfortable for them as individuals.

Gale, the mother of a fifteen-year-old, reported: "Lisa is slightly overweight, as are some of her girlfriends. She agonizes over her weight, and I hear endless hours of phone conversations about weight, diets, foods, weigh-ins, what they ate that day and so on. Several times when Lisa became upset about her weight, she asked me to help her 'stay on a diet.' I am supposed to buy lots of fruits and vegetables and keep all sweets out of the house. She asks me to stop her if I see her overeating. We go along in this pattern for a few days. Then comes a day when Lisa goes to the refrigerator and keeps nibbling, and I mention it to her like she asked me to, and she gets really angry and sarcastic. 'How dare you tell me what to eat! This is my house and my refrigerator, too. You're not the only one who lives here. Stop bothering me. I just want to eat!' What am I to do? When I don't comment about her eating, she accuses me of not caring if she gets 'fat as a house,' or if she becomes the most unpopular girl in school because she is fat. I feel damned if I do and damned if I don't."

What does Lisa want? Lisa is concerned about her weight, but she is also struggling with issues of dependence, authority and control. Food and eating can become one of the vehicles for parent and child to play out these issues. Lisa wants to be acceptable to her peers and ultimately to the adult world in terms of body size. But she is unsure how to get there or whether she can do it on her own.

It was crucial that Gale disengage herself from the attempt to regulate Lisa's eating. We suggested that she say, "I will not help you diet or help you put yourself down. You can be in full charge of your own eating." Giving Lisa this power removed food and weight issues from the developmental battleground.

Your child's way of dieting may be to monitor his food intake more subtly. A teenager will sometimes secretly count calories, devise his own diet, or go on one of the countless publicized diets. When you get an inkling that your child is eating in a regimented or artificially prescribed way, it is time to discuss the ramifications.

The most important message to give to any dieting child is that diets do not work! Why don't they? Diets do not take into consideration physical hunger. They ignore the reasons for overeating and the meaning of extra weight.

Diets are prisons. Like a prison inmate who is told what to do and when to do it, you are told when to eat, what to eat and where and how to eat it. As a prisoner, you are deprived, your menu never contains the foods you would choose for yourself, and the quantity is never enough.

That's just the point—you are supposed to suffer because you committed a crime: Either your appetite is out of control, and/or you think your body size does not conform to the ideal standard of the day. The response to deprivation in prison is often rebellion; so, too, is the response to food deprivation. Your rebellion is a binge—you eat all the "forbidden" foods you can get your hands on. As you eat, you say nasty things to yourself. The labels are endless: "pig," "slob," "wild," "out of control." Calling yourself names is an attempt to curb the binge, but it doesn't do that; it only leads to more binging. When you become totally disgusted with yourself, you once again take on the job of prison warden and place yourself back on the diet with the hope that *this* time it will be different. But, unfortunately, *it never is different.* You simply begin the diet-binge syndrome again.

Teenagers should be told that very few people succeed on

a diet unless they stay on it forever. Between 90 and 98 percent of dieters, once off the diet, gain back the lost weight plus a little extra each time. This means that only a very low percentage really succeed. The evidence is overwhelming that dieting is a no-win approach for everyone except the diet industry.

Adolescents often believe that other people know better than they "how to do it." Like other dieters, they allow themselves to be guided by the so-called experts, who know nothing about who they are, what they like or what they do. It's important to explain to your children what it feels like to be addicted to dieting. Let them know how hard it is to give up dieting and get back the inner control and authority to deal with eating and weight on your own terms. With self-demand feeding, you avoid diets and ensure a comfortable, relaxed and healthy relationship to eating and to your body.

To help Lisa's mother get her daughter off the diet track we compiled the following questions to be explored:

- Does Lisa feel her physical hunger? What is it like? Are different hungers connected to different foods? Does she sometimes eat when she is having an emotional need?
- Has Lisa noticed her pattern of overeating and binging after she has been on a diet for a few days? What does she think it was about? Does she understand that deprivation leads to binging?
- Does Lisa recognize how bad she feels about herself when she overeats? Does she call herself nasty names?
- What does the scale tell her? Are there other ways in which she could assess her body size and body fluctuations?

Lisa's mother needs to assure her daughter that adolescence is normally a time of growth spurts as well as weight and body changes. Self-criticism is not only pointless, it will make her feel worse and probably eat more. She could remind Lisa that a change in body size may be temporary and not a reason to panic or turn to artificial weight control. She could also help Lisa focus on her other attributes separate from body size and could explain to her that weighing herself constantly is not the way to decide whether she's "good" or "bad." It leads to eating by the numbers rather than from physical hunger. Dieting and weight are a "hot" topic for Lisa and her friends, and Lisa's desire to be part of the peer group may intensify her weight and dieting obsession. Her mother can suggest that Lisa talk with her friends about this new approach to eating and weight control.

If parents are attuned to some of the underlying causes of overeating and weight gain, they can begin to help their teenagers. Being attuned means helping your child move at his own pace, whether he is learning to walk or learning to be an adult. If you can have respect for his individuality and the particular emotional problems that he is facing at this age, you will be able to help him. However, if you feel that your child is a failure for not dating, for not being on the team, for not being more independent, he will know it. You will not be able to help him. In fact, his anger at your lack of support or understanding can be another impetus for rebellion and self-destructive conduct. Teenagers need permission to move at their own pace. An adolescent not yet ready to date should take her time; a teenager who does not excel in sports can have other areas of expertise. Teenagers need to know that they can go out into the world in their own way, at their own speed, and not lose your support and concern.

If you see your teen turn to food in an unnatural way, explore what is going on. Introduce her to self-demand feeding. The self-demand feeding approach will set you and your child on the right track. If you use it early enough, it will prevent eating problems from occurring. It will establish a lifelong habit of healthy and pleasurable eating as well as a self-sustaining comfort in one's own body. When older children with eating difficulties switch to the new program, they will eat in response to physical rather than emotional cues—and will be a lot happier for it.

III

SPECIAL PROBLEMS

13

FOOD ABUSE: ANOREXIA, BULIMIA AND COMPULSIVE OVEREATING

Teenagers who turn to food for emotional comfort have no natural restraint upon their appetite. Because they are not eating out of physiological hunger, they don't feel full. Though most children in this situation do not have long-lasting or pathological problems, some of them, particularly girls, *do* develop serious eating difficulties. They abuse food in much the same way other substances are misused.

The three most common forms of food abuse are anorexia, bulimia and compulsive overeating. A young girl who is *anorectic* will refuse to eat—she will actually starve herself. She has a distorted view of her body; she feels that she is too fat even though she may be wasting away. A *bulimic* is usually of normal weight but she will binge on huge quantities of food and then rid herself of it by vomiting or using laxatives or diuretics. A *compulsive overeater* will also eat huge quantities of food but will gain weight in the process and then diet to lose this weight.

How can you tell if your child is in danger of serious food abuse? You don't have to become a sleuth or detective, eying your teenager's movements and suspiciously looking for signs of a disorder. However, there are some clues to be alert to: If your daughter is constantly asking whether she's thin enough, or if you find food missing regularly, or if she's frequently in the bathroom after meals, it's time to explore whether you're seeing the beginnings of food abuse. The next question is, "Has the dialogue that once went on between my child and me stopped?" Have you been talking with her about her schoolwork, her friends, her feelings about dating, or have you been concentrating on looks, food and weight recently?

Some of the symptoms of food abuse are similar to what normal teenagers experience. It can be very difficult to sort out whether your child has a severe eating problem or is just having a difficult—normal—adolescence. Depression, rebelling against parents, unusual eating patterns and dieting are typical of the teenage years. What you need to watch out for is the combination and intensity of these behavior changes. These changes are likely to be more extreme with a pre-anorectic, bulimic or compulsive overeater than with a normal adolescent.

Anorexia*

PREOCCUPATION WITH THINNESS

The pre-anorectic girl, like most teenagers, is very much concerned with whether she's doing okay. She looks to the world to find that out. She asks people who are close to her about her weight as a way to do that. She feels deficient and thinks, "If only I were thin, and therefore perfect, things would be different." The pre-anorectic child is quite sensitive to the needs of others, particularly her parents. She tries to satisfy them by transforming herself, even though they may not particularly want her to be thin. When she asks, "Do you think I'm thin enough?" the most helpful response a parent can offer is, "I think you're just fine as you are. Is something bothering you at school, at home, with your friends?" This kind of attitude may alter drastically the progress of anorectic symptoms. The preanorectic might then choose an outlet other than her body to express her inadequate feelings.

*Miriam Gilbert contributed helpful information on her work with clients suffering from anorexia.

144

DEPRESSION

The pre-anorectic has sudden mood shifts that seem to come from nowhere and that are bewildering because nothing has drastically changed in the teenager's life. Her grades are the same as ever, her girlfriends constantly call and nothing has altered in the family. Yet the adolescent talks rudely to her parents. She throws temper tantrums, is argumentative and may be particularly jealous of and angry at her siblings. She may read a lot about death. Her rage seems all-consuming and gets you angry at the same time that it pushes you away. Perhaps you reason that she's just going through a phase and that if you let her alone, she'll get over it. Wrong!! Don't let her alone. Find out what's at the bottom of this new behavior; go for professional help if you can't talk with her.

STRIVING FOR PERFECTION

Her marks are very good, and she's been a popular girl, but now you hear grumblings of, "My grades aren't high enough." "No one likes me." "I'm really not like the others." She is anxious about her schoolwork, her appearance and her popularity, as she strives to be the best. She seems to have a frantic need for approval as well as to be nurtured and cared for. She thinks that by being "perfect," she will get what she craves and needs. Parental pressure and/or encouragement to perform better should be minimized. Try to give her the nurturing, independent of her skills and looks.

BEHAVIOR CHANGES

The pre-anorectic may begin to oppose her parents in ways not seen before; for example, you plan a surprise fiftieth-birthday party for your husband, and your daughter doesn't come. Or if she does show up, she brings a boy with her of whom you totally disapprove. This acting-out behavior spills over to many areas of your life together. Most significantly she begins to alter her usual eating patterns. She now wants to eat alone. And she certainly doesn't want you telling her what to eat; quite the reverse, she may cook meals and elaborate desserts for you and coax you to eat while she watches. She prefers raiding the refrigerator at night, alone. If you suddenly begin to find a lot of food missing regularly from your refrigerator, be alert to what's happening. She may be binging at night.

AMENORRHEA

This symptom may not be picked up by the parent. It is often the gynecologist who finds out that an adolescent's menstrual periods have stopped, even though her weight has not yet dropped to a dangerous level. Thirty percent of anorectics stop menstruating before drastic weight loss occurs.

PARENTAL CHANGES

You may find yourself constantly arguing with your spouse over what your daughter is doing. There may be disagreements over what she wears, her makeup, her choice of friends, her boyfriend, how she talks to you, what chores she's responsible for doing and so forth. Often the mother in the family feels unusually anxious. Rely on your own feelings about the shifts that are occurring in your family. Trust your belief that something is not as it once was and start talking about these feelings. First talk with your mate and then talk with your daughter.

If your child is pre-anorectic and communication is difficult, you will need to get professional help. Psychotherapy for the whole family, as well as for the child, is generally recommended. With outside help, the family dialogue can be resumed and the real issues addressed.

Bulimia

Ninety-five percent of all bulimics are women. Of these, most start the syndrome of binging and purging at eighteen, later than anorexia begins. Bulimia is also more easily hidden: The young woman's weight doesn't drop drastically and may seem quite normal.

Often a young woman becomes bulimic simply because she hears about it. Jo Ann told us, "I learned how to throw up from my roommate in college during my freshman year. At first I thought it was a gas. I could eat as much as I wanted and then get rid of it all just by putting my finger down my throat. It worked so well that whenever I ate too much, I would throw up. Before I knew it, I was eating huge quantities and purging.

All of a sudden it became a habit I relied on and was hooked on. Nothing could stop me."

A sixteen-year-old reported, "My sister and a group of her friends who work at the local ice-cream stand would always stay after closing time. Once I met them after work and I couldn't believe my eyes. They would have eating orgies and then go into the bathroom and throw it all up. I thought it was a great way to eat whatever you wanted and never gain an ounce."

For some girls, bulimia is a temporary problem, almost a rite of passage; for others, it becomes a way of life. Girls who are involved in activities like modeling, dancing or acting are often expected to maintain a slimness that is unnatural for growing bodies. Extreme methods of weight control, such as bulimia, unfortunately become the order of the day. One mother we know pulled her very talented daughter out of dance class when the youngster was told she had to watch her diet because weight gain would ruin her chances. Of course any healthy twelve-year-old should be putting on weight, not controlling her eating.

The binging and purging syndrome can consume many hours of the day. Yet it may remain undiscovered, since, for most bulimics, it is an activity filled with shame and carried out in secrecy. One college student told us that when she returned home one vacation, she confessed to her younger sister that she was bulimic. To her surprise her sister, with whom she was very close, told her she had been binging and purging for years.

Even though her eating is secretive, there are signs to look for:

- Large quantities of high-calorie foods are missing from your refrigerator, even though your daughter is not gaining weight.
- Money is missing from your wallet or your daughter is caught stealing. Remember that a bulimic may need a lot of money to support her food habit.
- The youngster goes to the bathroom after every meal and spends an inordinately long time there. Some bulimics run the shower while they're vomiting so that you don't become suspicious. If your daughter seems to take

an unusual number of showers or spends a lot of her time in the bathroom *after eating,* there is particular reason for concern.

- Some bulimics are quite impulsive. They may have a hard time organizing schoolwork. They seem scattered, change friends often and lose jobs. They may also be involved with drugs and drinking to excess.
- Dieting and breaking diets can be part of the repertoire. A bulimic is on a diet one moment and into the refrigerator the next. When you ask her about this, she may fight with you and tell you it's none of your business.

MEDICAL SIGNS

Though not all bulimics have the following symptoms, frequent vomiting may cause them:

- Bloodshot eyes from burst blood vessels
- Nosebleeds
- Constant sore throats
- Intestinal problems such as abdominal pain, diarrhea, spastic colon or constipation
- Swollen salivary glands, which may show up as puffiness under the jaws
- Severe tooth-enamel decay

Compulsive Overeating

Some teenagers turn to food and *overeating* as a way of trying to cope with or avoid the insecurities of adolescence. Your teenager feels scared, lonely and confused and she turns to food in an attempt to recapture the sense of nurturance and protection that she felt in childhood. What better way to recreate the comfort of babyhood than to fill up? The teenager soothes, even drugs herself, with constant feeding that eventually leads to her weight gain.

Signs that compulsive eating is becoming a problem might include the following:

- She may become less active or sluggish. Your teenager is not eating with physical hunger. She has just eaten a big meal, even had second or third helpings. Yet she continues to pick at leftovers or turns to snacks—seemingly nonstop. She eats when she is sad, happy, angry, scared. Food seems to punctuate all activities and feelings.

- She is getting fat. She goes on diets, loses a good deal of weight and then proceeds to regain it. Her weight goes up and down by many pounds.
- She is eating furtively; you find food missing. She is stashing food away; you find food wrappers in the wastebasket, in her drawers, in her pockets.
- Food and eating have become an obsession, taking up your teenager's time and mental energy. Her first thoughts in the morning, although she may not be really hungry, are about food, "What can I eat?" "What's in the fridge?" "What will I be having for lunch?"

For many teenagers, the weight gain itself can be used to avoid dealing with certain of the trials of adolescence. Marlene is thirteen and doing well in school. She is bright and pretty, although she hates the braces she has to wear on her teeth. She had a few close friends, but when they began to date, she withdrew from activities outside the home and spent much of her time eating. She is now overweight. "I feel really shy with boys and I get very nervous talking to them. My friends seem much more comfortable and they go to parties, dances and shows with them. Anyway none of the boys seem to like me that much. Sometimes they talk to me about their troubles with my friends, but I don't get asked out."

Marlene's story is typical. Over the last few decades, the pressures to begin dating and to become sexual seem to be starting earlier and earlier. For girls, adolescence is a time of learning to be attractive to others, especially boys. This frightens many youngsters who are not ready. Often, the onset of obesity during adolescence is a way of fending off sexuality. One of the most reliable ways of taking oneself out of the dating game is to get fat. The eating also helps pass time and is comforting and nurturing in the face of fears and loneliness.

For boys, adolescence is a time of consolidating athletic and intellectual achievements as well as dealing with sexuality. Like girls, adolescent boys may step back from the demands upon them by gaining weight. One father said, "Howard, our thirteen-year-old, is changing his eating habits. He doesn't want to eat with us but he spends hours before and after mealtimes snacking. We buy his clothes in the husky-boy department, which he hates, but that doesn't slow down his eating. He was always small for his age, and when sports became the major activity among his friends, he was chosen last for the team, if chosen at all. So sports were out as an area in which he could achieve and so was dating because most of the girls are much taller. With all this, he spends more and more time at home eating."

Weight gain can also communicate the message, "I'm not going to look the way you want me to look. I don't accept your ideals, your standards or your control over me." Teenagers are notoriously nonconforming and they can use their body size and physical attributes to express rebellion. Busily trying to figure out who they are, adolescents often feel that rejecting the norm is a prerequisite for establishing their own identities. For some overweight teenagers, their fat is a statement of their individuality, their refusal to conform. Parents can encourage their teenagers to express their uniqueness in other ways, not through eating and weight. Self-demand feeding is not only curative, it is preventative.

14

SPECIAL SITUATIONS

Very often in workshops where we present the self-demand feeding approach, parents ask how to modify our method to fit in with medical restrictions on their child's eating or with religious or moral constraints on the family's food choices. Following are some ideas on how best to handle these special situations.

QUESTION: We are vegetarians. How can we implement self-demand feeding when our child is not allowed to eat meat?

RESPONSE: There are many adults who have chosen a style of eating based on a particular philosophy. Your religion, moral or particular health concerns can define what is allowed in your diet and what isn't. Naturally, your child will be schooled in your way of thinking. The food restrictions you impose will be in concert with how you live your life. Just as we wouldn't say to someone who keeps a kosher home, allow your child to eat nonkosher foods, we wouldn't tell you to give your child meat if she wants it. However, you need to be alert to the potential use of the restriction as a basis for struggle that is really unrelated to the food-choice issue. In other words, when

Mandy says, "I went to Hilary's house and ate a hot dog," you need to explore with her the reasons behind this behavior. Did she just want to taste the hot dogs? Did she want to be like Hilary and eat what she was eating so that she wouldn't stand out? If she wanted to taste the meat because it was forbidden, you need to explain again why you are a vegetarian.

It is best not to make a big issue of this one incident. You can explain to your daughter all the ways in which she *is* already like her friend. You can tell her that no matter how similar people are, there must also be differences. Let her know that children are raised differently and that one way in which she *is* different is that she doesn't eat meat and Hilary does. You might also talk to her about how she can explain to others what eating rules she observes and why she observes them. Tell her some good and easy substitutes for the foods she cannot have and, perhaps, send them along when she visits. Pay particular attention to express these ideas at a level your child can understand.

This child has to learn that her family's way of eating *does* set restrictions on her range of choices. She needs to accept this; but she can still be free to make decisions about when, what and how much to eat within those prescribed boundaries. Some parents who are vegetarian cook vegetarian substitutes for meat dishes that their children love and that leave them without any feeling of deprivation. As long as the child can make food choices among a wide-enough range of basic nutrients and tastes, she should have no difficulty in meeting her particular internal cues of hunger.

QUESTION: What about the real deprivation that occurs with a child who is diabetic, allergic, or asthmatic?

RESPONSE: There are chronic conditions that require parental vigilance in terms of food and diet. Some illnesses and allergies demand that children not eat certain foods or that they eat particular foods in prescribed quantities. In these situations children can't choose from the full range to meet their hunger needs. Even with these limitations, however, self-demand feeding can be a part of these children's lives.

Recently we attended a meeting of parents with allergic and asthmatic children. It was instructive and quite moving to hear how these parents and their children handle the food restrictions with which they must live. Clearly, for an allergic or asthmatic child, diet plays an extremely important role in the control of and recovery from the disease. These parents were very aware of what foods would trigger an allergic response in their children. Most impressive were the reports about the children's own sensitivity and awareness, which often started at an early age.

One couple talked about their fourteen-month-old son, James, who was recently diagnosed allergic to corn and corn by-products. A month prior to learning this they took James to visit his grandparents. His grandfather gave him a lollipop. James took one lick and, to everyone's surprise, made a face and dropped it on the floor. The lollipop contained corn syrup, and if he had continued to eat it, he would have been very sick. Young as he was, his body gave him a message.

A parent of a five-year-old took his child, Steve, to a health food store. Steve selected a candy bar that had a picture of Superman on it. His father forgot to read the label, and when Steve took one bite, he proceeded to vomit it all up. He turned to his father, handed him the candy bar and said, "Read it." The label said it contained sesame, which Steve was highly allergic to. Of course, not all children will have an immediate physical response the way these two children did, but it is interesting to note how the body can, from an early age, signal what is or is not needed.

One mother of a ten-year-old told us that you really have to trust that your child is going to eat responsibly. We asked her what that meant. She said, "When my son, Paul, was quite young, I found out that he was asthmatic. Naturally, I was responsible for reading labels, shopping correctly and offering him foods that wouldn't harm him. I had to teach him, over time, to be as concerned, involved and knowledgeable as I was. After all, it is his body, and I was not going to be able to watch over his eating forever. I knew that when he went to school, began having sleepovers, going to birthday parties and so on, he would be on his own. I have learned that when a restriction is really necessary, children will follow it. They know what it feels like to be very sick. They don't want to have an allergic reaction to foods and end up in the hospital, so they learn what they can eat and what they can't."

Generally speaking, those around them have a harder time dealing with the deprivations than the children whose food is actually restricted. The stories unfolded: "Look, in the beginning when we were first confronted with all the things our Timmy couldn't eat, we were overwhelmed and depressed. Matter of fact, his grandparents kept referring to him as a 'poor thing.' I didn't know how I was going to prevent him from eating an ice-cream cone or having a piece of birthday cake. What I learned was that *I* was the one who was feeling deprived. Once I could get over my own feeling of deprivation, I was in a much better position to help Timmy."

Denial of the illness and excessive pity can interfere with helping your child find a way to eat that will be both satisfying and healthy. One woman said, "Our daughter was just diagnosed allergic to all corn products. My husband refuses to believe it and would not come with me to this meeting. He and my daughter have a ritual on weekends, they love to eat corn muffins for breakfast. Ralph says that he'll continue to let her eat as many corn muffins as she wants. What am I to do?"

This massive denial of the problem is fairly typical. The other parents advised the woman to explain to her husband that his denial can slow his daughter's recovery period and even prevent her from taking the necessary control over her body. If she is sensing her father's discomfort, she may decide not to pay strict attention to her new food needs. Concern for her father may override protection for herself.

This is not to say that there will never be a time when your allergic or diabetic child will feel deprived. As he begins to be aware of the limitations placed on his eating, this is bound to happen. You can help by having an honest, open discussion of the illness and of everyone's feelings about it. Your child needs to express what he feels about being different and having restrictions placed on him. And *you* need to talk, perhaps with other parents, about the worries you have and the work involved in caring for a child with special food needs. But in one way or another, restrictions and limitations are a part of life for many people. In the case of allergic and diabetic children these food restrictions are lifesaving. For other children different kinds of restrictions must be coped with, perhaps having nothing to do with food. Kids with ear problems have water restrictions, some children can't be exposed to the sun or are allergic to certain fibers, animals and so on. The issue is not so much the restriction but how it is handled.

In most cases the food restriction can be handled without creating undue deprivation and without interfering with the self-demand feeding approach. What is required for this method to work is that children be able to select foods to meet their specific hunger needs. The fact is that no parent can *always* meet the precise craving of her child. If the child wants hamburger and there is no hamburger meat in the house, something else will have to do. The trick, for the parent, is to find a substitute that will meet—or most closely meet—the child's hunger and that will feel satisfying. Sometimes this takes a little investigation into what is behind the specific demand. Does the child who asks for hamburger want something warm served on a roll? Will an egg or some other meat on a roll do the trick? Will ketchup on the sandwich help satisfy the particular appetite? Generally, if alternatives are discussed, an adequate one can be found or created.

The same process can work with an allergic child. For example, a child who is allergic to milk products asks for an ice-cream cone. You look for something that can be served in a cone that can provide the cool, sweet taste and even the creaminess of ice cream—ices, sherbets or frozen desserts made with soy or yogurt. Try to make as close a match as possible between the particular food choice and a permissible food.

One mother reported, "Each time Jason is invited to a birthday party, I call the parent giving the party in advance and find out what is being served. I then try to replicate the food using ingredients that my child is not allergic to. There are many good cookbooks to help me, including several specifically geared to people with food restrictions. The other day I made a delicious carob cake, which Jason took to his friend's party and ate while his friends ate the chocolate birthday cake. I've even learned to make icings out of ingredients that Jason can eat."

Within the framework of your child's restrictions, his food shelf should always be stocked with a wide variety of the foods he can eat. As long as he can choose from a range of foods with different nutritional elements and tastes like other children, he will be able to regulate his own food intake in a healthy and satisfying way.

Of course, these children, being no different than their nonallergic or nondiabetic counterparts, can use food as a weapon. The mother of nine-year-old Harold told this story: "Harold is deathly allergic to peanuts. The other night when I told him it was time to turn off the TV and go to bed, he said, 'If you don't let me stay up, I'm going to eat peanuts.' I told him he wasn't going to blackmail me in that way." Harold is no different from the child who says at bedtime, "I'm very hungry and thirsty, just let me eat and drink a little something and then I'll go to bed." Both children are using food to delay their bedtime and manipulate their parents. As we've said elsewhere in this book, an issue should not be made of the food in these confrontations. Deal instead with Harold's anger or the bedtime hour.

QUESTION: I have one child who is highly allergic and one who isn't allergic at all. Should I allow foods in the house that I know my allergic child can't have? Won't that be a terrible temptation?

RESPONSE: Yes, it will be a temptation. However, you can't restrict a child who is not allergic because his sibling is. For example, if one child is allergic to peanuts, is it fair to forbid her brother from having peanut butter? Your allergic child must learn to live in the world of food and say no to particular foods that make her ill. The family is a good place for her to learn this, in your presence and with your support. This doesn't mean that foods she can't have should be shoved under her nose. And you must be careful that the food restrictions don't get used as an expression of sibling rivalry. Just as an older child might use the fact that he can stay up later at night, the nonallergic sibling may use the fact that he can eat peanuts and his sister can't. This should be handled in the same way that all teasing is handled. And the allergic child should have as wide a variety of foods on her food shelf as her nonallergic brother has.

QUESTION: I refuse to buy foods that have additives and chemicals in them. My son has been bugging me about bacon. He was at someone's house for breakfast last week, and now all he wants is bacon. I don't want him to have nitrites. What do you suggest I do?

RESPONSE: There are really two ways to look at this. Our basic premise is that if particular foods weren't forbidden and therefore so enticing, children wouldn't have such a huge interest in them. Children would not be eating in response to restrictions placed but rather would eat food that their bodies needed and called for. They would eat with hunger and stop when full. Therefore, if your son knew he could have the bacon, he might be less interested in it.

But if your rule is "no bacon in the house," then he will have to do as he is told. Just remember that children can use anything to fight you. This may be the way your son has chosen to be defiant. Or he may be at an age where he needs to separate from you. When he takes a different stance than yours, he is expressing his own personality. You may want to evaluate whether you feel this is a definite and unchangeable no. As part of growing up, children must learn to accept the limits that you set. You, on the other hand, have to make the very hard decision as to which rules are absolute and inviolable and which are not. (You might also want to look into the bacon, now on the market, that is additive-free.)

Invariably, at the end of our talks with parents, someone will ask, "If we accept the idea that in some situations a child's food choices may be limited, then why should a parent's restriction on fattening foods be a problem? Why can't I use self-demand feeding and just not allow high-calorie foods in the house?" The answer is that this is a restriction based on two false premises: (1) the notion that high-calorie foods cause weight gain; and (2) that high-calorie foods are harmful and we must be afraid of them. If you prohibit foods for the purpose of staying thin, you are really saying that you are afraid of these foods. This is quite different than food limitations based on medical or philosophical concerns—these generally are not based on irrational fear.

If the goal is to prevent weight gain, you must understand that people gain weight because they overeat. In our experience, restrictions placed on high-calorie foods or sweets simply create a greater demand for, if not an obsession with, those foods. The inevitable response to the restriction is overeating

—binging—on the forbidden items when they become available. The chapters on sweets and dieting explain this point more fully. Restrictions on particular foods for the purpose of controlling weight is simply a form of dieting—it won't work.

A FINAL WORD

Until you try self-demand feeding, it is hard to trust the outcome. But try to think of what might happen if it did work: both you and your child would enjoy having all kinds of food available when you are physically hungry. There would be fresh fruits and vegetables, meats, whole-grains and dairy products—as well as candy sitting on the shelf and pints of ice cream in the freezer. No one would compete for any foods. Nothing would be a forbidden goody. Weight gain would not be the punishment for enjoyable eating.

The biggest hurdle to trying self-demand feeding may be the parents' fear of letting go of the reins and giving them to their child. Allowing your child to control his internal bodily needs is basic to his development. It is not neglect, nor is it anarchy, to let him be self-directed when it comes to his physiological needs. You can't make decisions for someone else's stomach. Just as you wouldn't tell your child when to go to the toilet, when to cough or when to sneeze, you can't tell him when he should be hungry or what he should be hungry for.

Over the years, we have seen families take the leap and begin to use self-demand feeding with their children. Once you're able to do that, you will be surprised by the excitement the approach generates in your family. It will actually be fun, and the struggles over food and eating that may have plagued your household will diminish.

Wouldn't it be nice if the next time you say to your child, "Don't spoil your appetite," you are really not trying to control his or her eating. Rather, what you are saying is, "Eat when you're hungry, eat foods of your own choosing, and stop when you are full." That is the essence of self-demand feeding. We wish you the best of luck and hearty appetites for all.

SUGGESTED READINGS

Bilich, Marion, *Weight Loss from the Inside Out,* New York, Seabury Press, 1983.

Brazelton, T. Berry, *Infants and Mothers,* New York, Dell Publishing Co., Inc., 1969.

———, *Toddlers and Parents,* New York, Dell Publishing Co., Inc., 1974.

Brody, Jane, *Jane Brody's Nutrition Book,* New York, Bantam Books, 1982.

Burck, Frances Wells, *Babysense,* New York, St. Martin's Press, 1979.

Eiger, Marvin S., and Olds, Sally Wendkos, *The Complete Book of Breastfeeding,* New York, Bantam, 1973.

Fraiberg, Selma H., *The Magic Years,* New York, Charles Scribner's Sons, 1959.

Hirschmann, Jane, and Munter, Carole, *Overcoming Overeating*, New York, Ballantine Books, 1989.

Kaplan, Louise, *Adolescence: The Farewell to Childhood,* New York, Simon and Schuster, 1984.

———, *Oneness and Separateness: From Infant to Individual,* New York, Simon and Schuster, 1978.

Leach, Penelope, *Babyhood,* New York, Alfred A. Knopf, 1983.

Leach, Penelope, *The Child Care Encyclopedia,* New York, Alfred A. Knopf, 1983.

———, *Your Baby and Child: From Birth to Age Five,* New York, Alfred A. Knopf, 1978.

McBride, Angela Barron, *The Growth and Development of Mothers,* New York, Harper & Row, 1973.

Orbach, Susie, *Fat Is a Feminist Issue,* New York, Berkley, 1978.

———, *Fat Is a Feminist Issue II,* New York, Berkley, 1982.

———, *Hunger Strike: The Anorectic's Struggle As a Metaphor for Our Age,* New York, Avon Books, 1986.

Polivy, Janet, and Herman, C. Peter, *Breaking the Diet Habit,* New York, Basic Books, Inc., 1983.

Roth, Geneen, *Feeding the Hungry Heart,* Indianapolis, Bobbs-Merrill Company, Inc., 1982.

———, *Breaking Free from Compulsive Eating,* Indianapolis, Bobbs-Merrill Company, Inc., 1984.

U.S. Department of Agriculture and U.S. Department of Health, Education and Welfare, *Nutrition and Your Health: Dietary Guidelines for Americans,* Washington, D.C., Government Printing Office, 1980.